# Teach
# on
# Purpose!

# Teach on Purpose!

## Responsive Teaching for Student Success

Leslie David Burns and Stergios Botzakis

*Foreword by Donna E. Alvermann*

TEACHERS COLLEGE PRESS

TEACHERS COLLEGE | COLUMBIA UNIVERSITY

NEW YORK AND LONDON

Published by Teachers College Press, 1234 Amsterdam Avenue, New York, NY 10027

Cover design by Sarah Martin. Cover photo by Rawpixel Ltd.

*Library of Congress Cataloging-in-Publication Data*

Names: Burns, Leslie D., author. | Botzakis, Stergios, author.
Title: Teach on purpose! : responsive teaching for student success / Leslie
    David Burns, Stergios Botzakis ; foreword by Donna E. Alvermann.
Description: New York, NY : Teachers College Press, [2016] | Includes
    bibliographical references and index.
Identifiers: LCCN 2016026989 (print) | LCCN 2016028504 (ebook) | ISBN
    9780807757888 (pbk.) | ISBN 9780807774922 (ebook)
Subjects: LCSH: Effective teaching. | Motivation in education.
Classification: LCC LB1025.3 .B9 2016 (print) | LCC LB1025.3 (ebook) | DDC
    371.102—dc23
LC record available at https://lccn.loc.gov/2016026989

ISBN 978-0-8077-5788-8 (paper)
ISBN 978-0-8077-7492-2 (ebook)

Printed on acid-free paper

Manufactured in the United States of America

23   22   21   20   19   18   17   16            8   7   6   5   4   3   2   1

# Contents

# Foreword

Before I had read a quarter of the way through *Teach on Purpose! Responsive Teaching for Student Success*, I knew this book was going to be different. It had the distinctive tone and substance of grit, well-placed humor, and sincerity. The authors—Les Burns and Stergios Botzakis, as well as the guest teacher-authors whom they invited as collegial chapter writers—are firmly united in their goal of engaging students first and foremost. They also make it clear that they expect their readers, whether other classroom teachers, administrators, parents, or teacher educators, to join them in their quest. They're serious and they write as if students' lives hang in the balance—because they do.

As I read further into *Teach on Purpose!* a strong sense of imagery took over. I imagined, though I know not whether this is purely a figment of my imagination, that Les Burns and Stergios Botzakis must have started this book back when they were classroom teachers. Granted, they may not have drawn consciously on what I envision as hastily written notes jotted down in a planner at the end of a long day spent teaching when more things went wrong than right. For if not this or some similar experience, how else could they have earned what I'm calling their compassion buttons—those imaginary keys on a laptop which, when tapped in a certain order, spell out what makes teaching difficult yet so compelling that one can't wait for the next day to get back at it for the kids' sakes?

Surely, too, the little warnings the authors have interspersed from time to time (such as, avoid teaching as if engaged in battlefield triage) fed my imagination as I pictured one or both of them winging a lesson and then coming close to panic at the sight of 25 pairs of eyes asking voicelessly, "Now what?" For it's in admitting to imperfection that we perfect our craft as teachers. This sense of becoming is in part what I imagine has made it possible for the authors to launch naturally into a discussion in Chapter 8 on ways of being responsive to students by asking sincere questions. When an invited teacher-author then moves the discussion from theory to practice in Chapter 9 with a unit plan on using sincere questions to teach imperialism in social studies, it becomes clear just how purposeful Burns and Botzakis have been in conceptualizing this remarkably fine book.

And, if I'm interpreting the authors' intentions correctly, it is in drawing upon their own previous and current experiences that they are able to write with such conviction about responsive teaching as a way of engaging students' funds of knowledge. In an increasingly globalized society that is built on shifting economic terrain—one in which families move back and forth across borders if not with physical ease, then certainly with virtual access through media and the Internet—teachers who welcome diverse funds of knowledge are in the know. Such welcoming, of course, carries with it the responsibility of teaching students to read and write critically. A classroom teacher–written chapter on "An Odyssey into Multiple Media" captures not only the how and what of such teaching, but also the why. Like the other three teacher-authored chapters in *Teach on Purpose!,* this one carries the thinking of Burns and Botzakis to new heights by illustrating the practicality of drawing on students' funds of knowledge.

As I reached the concluding chapter of this book, I realized just how effortless my journey had been. Not because what I had read was an easy and surface level text, or even known to me previously. Quite the contrary: In my opinion, the effortlessness I experienced was due to being thoroughly engaged from start to finish. More than once I stopped to argue with the authors (my sometimes-favorite stance as a reader), to highlight a particularly useful example that I wanted to include in my own teaching, to savor a humorous anecdote, or to draw an analogy in a different discipline (science, mathematics, English language arts, or social studies). For if *Teach on Purpose! Responsive Teaching for Student Success* were to accomplish nothing else, it will likely go down in publishing history as being a text that tells it like it is: Teaching *is* hard work, and not for the faint of heart, the romantic, or the techno-robotic posthuman. It is, however, the ideal profession for making a difference, as the authors of this book claim repeatedly.

*Donna E. Alvermann*
The University of Georgia
Athens, GA

# Acknowledgments

## From Stergios

Writing this book has been a long, challenging, fun, and rewarding experience, and I owe a great many people my gratitude. *Teach on Purpose!* has been a long-stewing labor of love between my main man, Les Burns, and me. Les, you are a true scholar, friend, and warrior, and I am lucky to know you. Regina Ward has been our editor, and I cannot think of a more thoughtful, patient, understanding, or helpful person to work with. I appreciate everything you have done to help us write the best book we can while also maintaining our sanity. You have been more kind and flexible than I deserve. I also would like to thank the following people for all their work: Emily Renwick, Nancy Power, Kate Bradford, Noelle De-La-Paz, and the fine folks at Teachers College Press, who have done much to ensure we were successful. I want to thank our contributors Katie Raby and Barry W. Golden for their fine work and for teaching me a thing or two (or eight!). I would like to thank my colleagues and students at the University of Tennessee, Knoxville, and elsewhere for all the wonderful academic discourse and support. I am extremely lucky to collaborate, teach, and be taught by you all. To my wife, Nora Vines, you are the sunshine that helps me grow and live, and I cannot put into words how much you mean to me. I love you to the moon and back, Princess Pineapple Chunk! And finally, to my son George, who was born midway through the writing of this manuscript. You have taught me patience and humility, and you are the best baby I could ever ask for. I cannot wait to see you grow up.

## From Les

I'm not sure it's possible to fully acknowledge all of the people who helped us make this book a reality. My coauthor, Stergios? Without you my life as a teacher and scholar would never have been such a joy, and writing this and so much more with you has made me a better teacher and thinker than I ever dreamed. You are a brother to me. I also thank my wife Colleen Burns for her inspiration and loving support, especially during the many moments

I curled up on the floor in panic and she helped me get back up and realize that not only could I write a book, I was meant to write *this* book. Colleen, I dedicate this to you, my wife the teacher. You have taught me more about how to live, love, and grow than I can ever repay. I can never love you back enough, but I'm damned sure going to try. Thank you to my family and friends who cheered us on. Wow to my amazing teacher colleagues Ryan New and Maureen Cavalcanti for their enthusiastic and brilliant work modeling what it means to be purposeful and responsive professionals. You two are going to change the world. I also want to acknowledge Renee Boss, the Fund for Transforming Education, and the Next Generation Instructional Design project teachers in Kentucky for inviting me to join their community and explore how to improve our work together. Thanks to Margaret Schroeder, Joseph Flynn, sj Miller, George Hruby, Leigh Hall, David Kirkland, Brandon Abdon, Ashley Lamb-Sinclair, and all my students and colleagues at the University of Kentucky. You inspired me, and inspire me still to get up every day and work to be a better educator and human being. Finally, thanks to our editor Regina Ward for her incredible generosity, wisdom, patience, kindness, and especially belief and trust that we could do this. Thank you for letting us labor with love.

# CHAPTER 1

# Introduction
## Teaching on Purpose

### BEING REAL ABOUT TEACHING

Let's acknowledge a few things before we get started. First, teaching is really, really, *really* hard work. It is not just that it isn't for the faint-hearted. We mean teaching will eat you for breakfast, suck the marrow from your bones, and pick its teeth with one of your ribs before finishing its first cup of very black coffee that morning. As Donald Quinn famously asserted, most people have no idea just how difficult teaching really is. Quinn (n.d.) suggests the following analogy:

> If a doctor, lawyer, or dentist had 40 people in his office at one time, all of whom had different needs, and some of whom didn't want to be there and were causing trouble, and the doctor, lawyer, or dentist, without assistance, had to treat them all with professional excellence for nine months, then he might have some conception of the classroom teacher's job.

We would love to watch the reality TV show where that was the premise.

Think teaching is easier than medicine, law, or scraping people's teeth with a steel hook? Okay, try doing what you do with smooth expertise while operating under the conditions actual teachers deal with every single day. Our point is that anyone who has spent even one day working in a classroom quickly realizes that teaching is much harder than it looks. People with such experience are also likely to notice that *good* teaching under normal conditions is an amazing, complex accomplishment that requires not just effort but serious, deep, professional expertise.

Teaching isn't only hard. It's complicated. Some scholars have suggested it doesn't take 10,000 *hours* to master the job, as Malcolm Gladwell (2008) made a lot of money claiming, but 10 *years*. That's 87,600 hours for those of us who fear math, and it's so much more complicated that we want to suggest to Mr. Gladwell that he be more careful about making such false claims in bestselling books sold to people who wish life was simpler. Ten thousand hours may get you started, but it won't make you an expert. It certainly won't save you when you face 180 students the first day of school and realize it is your responsibility to not just "manage" them but *teach* them enough so that they will be prepared for the lives they will lead after they leave school and become adults.

Teaching is so complex that, according to one landmark study (Danielson, 1996), teachers make over 3,000 nontrivial decisions *per day*—a mind-blowing level of work, revealing just how complex life in classrooms is. With 3,000 important decisions to make every day, a teacher who operates without a purposeful design for engaging students is bound to have trouble. And what teachers decide to do and say (or not) really matters to how well students learn. According to a recent study by the RAND Corporation (2014), teachers account for up to a mere 14% of the variables that affect how well (or how poorly) a student learns. That leaves up to 86% beyond the teacher's control, and that is quite scary enough, thanks. The larger body of studies documented by Berliner, Glass, and Associates (2014) shows that, at best, teachers *may* account for *up to* 30% of students' success, but even then our 30% maximum effect might not be the most important or largest variable at work. On top of that, a teacher's work and its effects on the students she teaches change from class to class, day to day, and year to year because of circumstances beyond *any* teacher's control. Bottom line? Teaching is among the most difficult jobs to do well in the history of humanity.

For example, how is anyone supposed to teach authentic reading and writing concepts, skills, and processes when you have a swarm of 45 students in class at one time because your school district thinks like a corporation and doesn't accept the well-established facts that teaching kids to read and write requires smaller class sizes, which result in accelerated learning success and higher standardized test scores (National Council of Teachers of English [NCTE], 2014)? When NCTE (1996) issued its first position statement on optimal class sizes for teacher success and students' literacy learning, it asserted no teacher should ever work with more than 100 students per year! Ah, to sleep. Perchance to dream. Alas. Forty-five students per class is now common, and 180 students per day in any classroom makes certain ways of healthy teaching . . . uh . . . less healthy.

Beyond the chaos that comes as a direct result of bureaucrats and school administrators too often treating your classroom like it's big enough to host a Justin Bieber concert, many if not most students do not come to class—no matter what subject you teach—simply because they love or even especially like your subject. They might, and you can help them learn to appreciate it, try it, and engage it to the point where they might even learn to like and love it. We're all good teachers and because we are passionate and spark their interests, every year we all reach students who insisted they wouldn't play along. But when they get to us in middle or high school, most of them don't come because they are moths to the seductive flames and beacons of enlightenment we shine. Some absolutely seek us out, and that's good. But others are placed in classes, at least sometimes, just because a class fits into their schedule, or because it is required by state law. Many and even most students are with us not really because they are motivated each day to race eagerly to school. Some do, no doubt. But others don't value what we are offering, for lots of different reasons, so along with high numbers we also have to deal with the fact that many of our students simply don't want to be with us. According to Guthrie et al. (2006), they became *demotivated* and actively learned to resist education.

## AIN'T NOBODY GOT TIME FOR THAT!

As most teachers have discovered, and as many may have felt themselves when they were students, kids often have good reasons to hate school. Just ask Pink Floyd about why they don't need no education, and they will kick up some seriously ominous and blackly honest answers: From where a lot of young people are standing, school sucks. Many perceive it as a waste of time or a rigged game they can't win.

We're talking to teachers and prospective teachers here. We understand that Paul Feig and Judd Apatow (2004) got it right when they made the TV show *Freaks and Geeks*. It's tough for most kids in the first place to thrive in school and grow up there, even when they seem tough, cool, sweet, or popular. It's still our job to help them and teach them, make them want to learn, and help them see that what we offer has value. That's what this book is about.

Because so many students do not see school as a place where anything especially worth doing gets done, part of the problem is helping them generate sincere motivations to join us in learning. For them, school is a place where they are closely monitored for behavior and forced to compete with peers in public ways that include published grades that categorize them into groups deemed (at least) "high," "average," and "general" (a repellent set of euphemisms that overtly label a majority of students as only capable of average or below average work). They are told to follow rules whether the reasons are clear or not; they are required to adhere to a preset schedule that doesn't always match up with their needs for nutrition, bathrooms, socializing, physical activity, stimulation, and more. On top of all that, they are required to constantly navigate classrooms in which they must do their best to fit in with other students who may not be like them and to please teachers whether that seems like a worthwhile thing to do or not (Jackson, 1990). Why?

Did you know school architecture is literally the baby of what must have been a spectacular love affair between prison architecture and the architecture of insane asylums (Smith & Burston, 1983)? It really was, and it still is. Jackson (1990) describes the effects this kind of environment is likely to have on any humans who enter it (including teachers), but he's rather dry about it because he's being a good scientist. We seek to be candid about his findings. Here is what he concluded, in part: Schools are built to house large populations, control them tightly, move them around as efficiently as possible, and monitor them to ensure that William Golding's (2012) *The Lord of the Flies* doesn't go beyond an allegory. Because of all that, because of tradition, because of standards, because of high-stakes standardized testing, because of value-added measures of teaching, because of the third rendition of Harry Wong's professional development program in 4 years, because of accountability and parent phone calls and email and the schedule and extra-curricular activities and ohmygodjuststopmakingsomanyannouncements! Whew!

On top of all that, the typical teacher (and student) these days gets only 20 minutes to eat lunch—along with 2–4 meetings each day (PLC, Dept, IEP, 504, SBDM, ARC, RTI). You used to have a "planning period" where you really could plan lessons and other instruction, or prepare and adjust what you were doing as a teacher. Now you have "common planning meetings" that are, to be generous, collaborative. Can they work? Yes. They can. We've seen them work beautifully. They really can leverage a group's collective knowledge and skills to strengthen the whole and come together, while maintaining respect for individuals' professional autonomy to teach in ways and using resources that are best for their particular students based on their professional judgments. When they work that way, they are powerful, wonderful, and even pleasurable. Sometimes such professional communities even look into new or alternative methods and developments in knowledge so they can be sure they are up to date on contemporary teaching for their content areas. They go to conferences together to see what other people are doing that they can take back and use with their own students.

But many collaborative teacher groups labeled "professional learning communities" function more like assembly lines where "common" plans are made and where "common" assessments are created to make sure the curriculum aligns with whatever tests the students will be required to take. Teachers in these groups agree on what texts to teach, how they will connect those texts to standards for compliance with accountability systems, which skills and concepts they will teach, when they will teach them (sometimes down to the date), and who will create which graphic organizers, PowerPoint slides, guided note packets, formative assessments, and rubrics to make sure everyone has the same content, format, information, sequence, and timeline. That's tedious and often contentious work, it eats time, and it sucks meaningful individualized instruction out of classroom work—when meaningful work is the key to success.

Then teachers have to face their students. The students are . . . a little ticked off many days, downright grumpy even, and often for good reasons. Much of the time they are upset, angry, sad, or agitated for reasons we may never know. Worse, we might misinterpret their frustrations and assume they are angry with us, then treat them in kind because we are humans with feelings who don't feel good when the people we are trying to help resent us for it. They might not be able to tell us why they are unhappy, not least because they are not yet psychologically mature or cognitively developed enough to identify, understand, and tell us why they feel certain ways at certain times. They're just kids. We must remember that even high school seniors are still more children than young adults, even as we treat them with as much respect and dignity as possible.

Because they are not yet mature, or because they are confused about what is supposed to be going on in school, or because they have disabilities, or because they are bored, young people often act out in negative ways. They misbehave. They refuse to work. They sleep. They flirt. They pick on one another. They try to get you to go off on tangents. They are distracted. Let's not even get into the paper load many teachers have to carry and grade in order to make sure each student gets helpful, authentic feedback to learn from, or the home visits and parent nights that are as much about public relations as good teaching. And there are—lest we forget—test preparation and testing duties. According to Nelson (2013), students spend as many as 150 hours or more per school year just preparing for and completing standardized tests. That's over 10% of a school year spent practicing for and completing standardized tests that are not truly used to help the students who take them. And that is insane.

## TEACHING AS TRIAGE

So teaching is often about triage (Green, 2014)—deciding in the midst of action which matters and tasks are most pressing at any given moment. In war, *triage* is the term used to describe the process of deciding which wounded soldiers need medical help first, and which should be able to live long enough to wait and still survive. Triage is not an ideal model for medical care, and it's certainly not healthy for education. We plan down to the minute but often are forced to put plans aside and spend all our time doing triage instead. When we do, and if that triage scenario is allowed to dominate, we reduce our attention to the real education we sought to implement as professionals. We even forget that we became teachers for important reasons that had nothing to do with meeting standards or complying with test requirements. We stand in the hubbub of our classrooms and schools, and we forget we're there because education matters and *means* something. Education has purposes. They are noble purposes, and it is our job as professionals to engage them purposefully. We teach because education is all about helping our students learn, grow up, and make sense of the amazing, cool, incredible world they live in now. You know the world we mean. It's the one we plan to trust them with when we are gone. We teach because we want them to make their world for themselves and then care for it in ways that make everyone and everything better—as much as we can, all the time.

When we get caught up in triage teaching (Green, 2014), we forget we are there to teach and learn all the fascinating things there are about the world, how to live in it well, how to make it better, how to overcome the errors of our ways, how to be better people, and how to help everyone succeed. Do we want Utopia? Yes! Yes, we do. No, we don't think it's an actual possibility. No, we don't believe it's possible to sustain an absolutely perfect society. But! We do believe people can, should, and ought to learn the ideals of such a society and strive for them. Like Sisyphus, we should roll that rock up the hill over and over again every day (with no small amount of joy for the privilege), working in both small and large ways to make things better than they are now for as many people as possible. If we don't want to do that work, why do we bother pretending to be teachers at all?

But we forget sometimes. We forget it while we flip out under the pressure to get students college- and career-ready. We get caught up in the sidetracks of preparing them for the next battery of tests that will be used by people who have little idea about how our jobs work yet evaluate whether we are successes or failures. But what we forget is not hard to remember. It is powerful stuff. We can overcome all of that if we teach on purpose.

What we really mean when we say things like, "All students should be prepared for college and career by the time they graduate from high school," is that we want our society's youth ready for life as they will know it. We can do that. We're professionals. We're teachers. We are members of the profession that creates all other professions, and we matter.

## A BETTER WAY:
## TEACHING ON PURPOSE WITH STUDENTS AT THE CENTER

In this book, we talk about how to help teachers in all content areas be systematically and purposely successful by, first of all, responding to students instead of forcing them to comply with a system that assumes they can, should, ought, or will become like us for their own good, like it or not, how we say, when we say, where we say, and why. In this book, we talk about what matters: the students, *their* worlds, and how to teach them in meaningful ways on purpose so that they become prepared for the day when we will not be here to do it all for them. We are going to talk about how to put meaning back into our work and make teaching about more than school. None of us teaches "school." We teach *students*, and we teach them how to learn and live good lives. We teach them to make themselves and the worlds they will live in. It's not the world we helped make and live in now, although that's a part of it. We are trying to prepare them for the version of the world they are revising before our eyes right now—the one *they* are going to live in when we are gone.

Most teachers assume that future society isn't going to be like ours. As Bruce (2002) wrote, "We have trouble conceiving that we could become something other than what we are today" (p. 15). In aspects of the world that remain familiar, there will be odd currents and unpredictable shifts that change how things look, how our students think, and why they do what they do in life. In still other ways, changes to the world as we know it now will be so radical even our students cannot begin to describe or explain how society will be, how it will work, or what people will need from education to live in it well.

We're going to talk in this book about how to teach well. A lot of what we know to be good educational practice for diverse students in contemporary society is hard work, highly resisted by people who do not understand it, or just plain impossible in the face of the nuttiness that passes for a typical day in public school.

There was no Golden Age when teaching and school were simple and perfect. When the United States started comparing its schools with those of other nations back in the 1950s, there were 12 different countries participating in the comparison. We placed 11th. We've never been #1, in anything, since the start of that whole investigation. We aren't #1 now. We would be, though, in every single category, if the measures they were using accounted for just one more variable—poverty. But the comparisons don't control for poverty, so we are told by those data that we are failing (Berliner et al., 2014). We should punch those data right in the face. As Berliner et al. find, they're wrong because international comparisons of school, teacher, and student quality are based on flawed constructs that miss what they claim to measure. But it helps highlight what we are saying here: Teaching is hard work worth doing. Being purposeful can help make your job easier, more pleasurable, and more meaningful and valuable to your students. We cannot know exactly what the future holds. But we can do our jobs using knowledge on purpose, and we can teach in ways we know are right and good for everyone in ways that make teaching less about triage and more about triumph.

There is science to what we do in teaching, and art. Using our professional knowledge, we can ask more-sincere questions and respond to who our students are in ways that help ensure that, whatever the future holds, we prepare them to know, think, do, and believe in ways that matter. We know how to make students want to learn. We know proven methods for increasing classroom success. We know teachers can help students learn and make sense of the world, even as the world continues to change. We do that now, and we know you can too. The question we must all ask ourselves constantly is: *Are we responding to our students and teaching on purpose?*

## TEACHING AND IDEALISM

Teaching in the ways advocated for in this book requires idealism. Count-less teachers have been labeled idealists, and their *idealism* is a quality to desire and pursue. An idealistic teacher never stops refining and growing and never settles. In teaching, there is no magic key that unlocks it all for us and makes education simple. Excellence in teaching means constantly adapting, changing, growing, and expanding with as much purpose and awareness as possible in order to continue getting as close to perfect as you can. You know you can never achieve perfection because—remember—as a teacher you've got at least 70 to 86% of the things around you happening completely outside your control. Still, purposeful teachers should be ideal-ists. Idealism means the eternal pursuit of excellence. It is fundamental to the profession.

Les has been an educator for 20 years, and Sterg for 18 years. We each spent 5 of those years teaching high school and middle school. We both worked with students of all ability levels from diverse socioeconomic and cultural backgrounds. For the remainder of that time, we both studied the fields of education, curriculum, policy, literacy, and, especially, teaching and teacher education in depth, earning master's and doctoral degrees and even-tually becoming university professors. For the past 11 years Les has chaired the teacher certification and degree programs for all English educators at one large flagship state university, and Sterg has coordinated content-area reading curriculum and directed the middle school program at another. We have had unique opportunities as professionals to present and publish in national forums, author national standards, help lead local and national professional organizations, and, of course, work with many people on their ways to becoming professional teachers too.

Les moved from high school to college in 2000, and Sterg moved from middle school to college in 2002. We both made that move in the middle of one of the largest reform efforts in U.S. history: the renewal of the Ele-mentary and Secondary Education Act (ESEA), which became known as No Child Left Behind (NCLB) in 2001, which was rebranded under the Obama administration as Race to the Top and as of 2010 branded yet again as the Common Core State Standards Initiative, most recently revised in late 2015. Based on our experiences preparing new professionals, coaching them, and supporting teachers at work since NCLB and the Common Core, we have found that teachers have far less freedom to exercise professional judgment than we did less than 20 years ago.

That autonomy we had mattered. A lot. It mattered because as profes-sionals with extensive expertise, we were able and especially *allowed* to keep track of what our students knew, how well they were learning, what they would best learn next, and how that learning would lead to success as young adults entering the broader world. We made plenty of mistakes and miscalculations as we honed our skills and often had to work hard to refine those skills so that we truly could make a difference. But we remember countless "Aha!" moments we experienced with our students—deeply moving lessons we were allowed to pursue when we all came together and worked to make sense of what we studied. We collaborated with our colleagues to meet the needs of specific students and coordinated instruction across various curricula. We certainly taught and covered plenty of traditional content: knowledge, strategies, skills, concepts, and more. But the most exciting, important, and valuable learning happened when we responded to our students and spent time talking about what the things we read and wrote meant to *them*, why our content mattered to *them* as people, and how to *use* what we learned to make sense of ourselves and the world around us.

As English teachers, we used novels like *The Catcher in the Rye* (Salinger, 2008) to explore what it means to be young and face the frightening uncertainties and sometimes harsh realities of growing up. We read short stories like Alice Walker's "Everyday Use" (1973) in connection with our own experiences to understand that a person's identity doesn't come from what she hangs on her wall but what she *makes* and *does* in life. We read, viewed, and performed *Julius Caesar* to explore how power can corrupt, and how good intentions can have tragic consequences. We wrote about all those topics, every day and every week, but we also wrote about ourselves and our own lives in relation to those topics. We used narratives, reports, poetry, and other genres to explore our values and beliefs, and we shared those explorations to broaden our perspectives about the ways people can see and be in life. Our experiences helped us learn that teaching is a useless project unless it is connected to topics, themes, concepts, and ideas that are *meaningful*.

Teaching adolescents is among the best ways of learning how to understand the world and live in it as a healthy, happy, productive, supportive, and successful human being. Many if not most of us became teachers specifically because we learned to love those moments of discovery, wonder, realization, and identification. They were thrilling. They were fun. They were interesting and relevant to us. They helped us think and grow on purpose instead of by accident, and we didn't just teach  to help students pass tests and get good grades. We taught because it mattered.

Somewhere between then and now, something went wrong. As teacher educators and teachers, we have spent the past 15 years observing novice and experienced teachers at work in their classrooms, studying methods with them, exploring proven strategies for increasing student success, and trying to improve and refine our professional tools and practices. We've observed hundreds of lessons, hundreds of teachers and students hard at work. And during those 15 years, we have witnessed a terrible loss—an unacceptable sacrifice. In the face of ever-increasing pressure to meet standards, ensure students score at "proficient" levels on standardized tests, and supposedly prepare children for college and work, our profession has lost much of what made it important in the first place. In the national quest to make sure teaching is *effective*, we lost capacity to make our teaching matter beyond school.

## PURPOSE MATTERS

This is a book about why meaningful, purposeful teaching matters in our schools both now and for the future. In November 2013, we presented a session at a national conference. We focused on how to design and teach lessons using multiple forms of media to help modern students engage more fully with traditional texts by also using multiple nonprint media. As we presented, something very exciting started to happen. Although we began a conversation about how to use books, videos, and graphic novels to help students learn standards-based academic concepts and skills, the teachers who attended our session began to veer into deep discussions about the meanings of the texts we were using to present. We had asked a single unifying question to create a common thread across those texts: "What happens when you try to control other people?" The teachers agreed using new kinds of text and multiple media beyond tradition in school was important. But we all discovered a much more important notion as a result of the conversation. By using that question—"What happens when you try to control other people?"—teachers from all over the country began to talk about how refreshing it was to actually explore what our subject matter *means*, why it matters, and how those meanings are either absent in their work now or becoming more and more difficult to pursue. Why? Because we have all been forced to use standards for academic achievement as the curriculum (rather than the outcome) to prepare our students so they score well on tests, without addressing why those tests matter, and we never really consider how useless they are in our real, messy, nonstandardized lives.

In this time of increased standardization, accountability, and standards-based education, how can we make sure our lessons and units are designed to be purposeful all the time? How can we help ourselves to be sure our teaching is consistently meaningful and useful? How can we ensure that we are helping *all* students engage fully in their own learning, reading, writing, talking, and thinking in ways that help them mature into successful adults, ready for the world? This book is our attempt to respond to those questions and reclaim the heart and soul of teaching: purposeful, sincere, and meaningful education about what life is and how to live it well for the good of everyone.

In Chapter 2, we explain what we call *responsive teaching*, an approach based on proven research-based knowledge that can be used in any content area at any grade level to improve teaching and learning. Chapter 3 explains how to build environments that support increased learning and meaning-making based on research about motivation and engagement. Chapter 4 describes how to collect and use data about students' identities to center our curricula and make principled decisions about how to teach in ways proven to increase student success. In Chapter 5 we offer our first Model Unit Plan, in mathematics, to demonstrate how data about students' identities and lives can be used to engage them in academic learning. Chapter 6 focuses on designing purposeful unit and lesson plans, including how to identify manageable learning targets, design formative learning tasks, sequence them, and implement plans in ways that maximize student success. We then offer a second Model Unit Plan for science instruction in Chapter 7 to show how instructional design sequencing can look. Chapter 8 describes how to create and use sincere questions, questions that both focus curriculum and position students to answer richly, variously, and successfully in order to drive instruction and support learning. A third Model Unit Plan follows, in Chapter 9, to demonstrate how such questions support purposeful instruction in social studies. Chapter 10 explains why use of multiple media formats is crucial for teaching adolescents in contemporary society, followed by a fourth Model Unit Plan in Chapter 11, from English language arts, to describe how such texts can be integrated in plans and enhance student engagement. We conclude in Chapter 12 by reviewing the content of the previous chapters and models, and exploring implementation opportunities. Drawing on that previous content, we explore how you can put it all together and can become a responsive teacher who works professionally, on purpose, at all times, in ways that are proven and pleasurable.

By teaching in responsive ways on purpose, teachers can use this book to meet any reasonable set of academic standards at any level, any time—whether they are the Common Core State Standards used today or new standards that almost certainly will be created in the future. Readers will learn to not just meet standards but exceed them. Let's do it on purpose.

# CHAPTER 2

# Responsive Teaching
## What It Is, Why It Matters

Most teachers teach responsively in at least some ways and often have studied it as part of their certification processes. For decades, teachers, teacher educators, and researchers have worked to figure out how to teach diverse students—students who are different from one another, whether in terms of race, ethnicity, economic status, culture, language, geography, sexuality, gender, or other variables. Key concepts in the field include *culturally responsive teaching* (Gay, 2010), *funds of knowledge instruction* (Moll & Gonzalez, 2001), and *third-space teaching* (Gutierrez, 2008). These add to the *constructivist* approach John Dewey (1938) outlined nearly a century ago.

When we talk about *responsive teaching*, we mean teaching that is purposeful, intentional, and explicitly designed to (1) help all students succeed at optimal levels, (2) create curriculum based on learners' identities *and* academic needs for success in school and society, (3) identify and select methods and learning tasks that leverage those identities and needs to increase learning, and (4) use the resulting data to sustain successful learning environments at the interpersonal, small-group, classroom, school, and community levels as consistently as possible in a system that we know is always changing along with the society it serves.

Responsiveness is an integral part of teaching on purpose. Because it's hard to plan for this type of teaching, we know that professionals have to compromise and adapt at least sometimes (perhaps a lot of the time), despite knowing that those compromises may detract from their highest ability to teach and provide their students' opportunities to learn. However, responsive teaching is the right thing for professionals to do because it helps teachers remain purposeful even when conditions threaten to push them to triage teaching. This chapter provides an overview of what responsive teaching looks like, why it matters, and how to think and work as a responsive professional educator.

## HOW WE GOT HERE: ONE SIZE FITS ALL

Public education and the way it has been designed as a system during the course of U.S. history have made it harder to be a responsive teacher than it should be, given what professionals have known about methods for successful education in public schooling since the late 19th and early 20th centuries. Without launching into a dense history, it's worth knowing there are some very real, longstanding approaches to education that have become so traditional that they've achieved a status of common sense—ideas that seem so obviously logical that we barely think about them, let alone consider whether they actually help us attain our goals and teach well. In the early 20th century, many educators sought to make teaching as scientific as possible. They borrowed certain models of efficiency and productivity from industrialism and corporatism. Two major influential models, Taylorism (Littler, 1978) and Fordism (Doray, 1990), are still recognizable, when one considers how they are still used today to determine how teachers do their work. The problem with these models is not that efficiency and productivity are generally undesirable. It's that the models for attaining those conditions were created in order to make *factories* more efficient and productive so that every single item produced would not only have the same quality, but would also be made in the *exact same way* using the same processes, steps, methods, and materials, no matter who was doing the job. Schools and classrooms are patently and emphatically *not* factories! They do not *produce* products *efficiently*. Classrooms are places that should be designed to systematically *educate* people *successfully*. Successful people are very different from efficiently produced products. And while it's understandable to wish that teaching people were as simple as producing cars or washing machines, that's not really a desirable goal for a democratic society in our contemporary, diverse, ever-changing world. So how did Taylorism and Fordism become so ingrained in our educational system, and how can understanding this help us work as teachers to do a better job? Let's explore how Taylorism and Fordism affect what we do in schools today.

## TAYLORISM, FORDISM, AND THE PROBLEM WITH "EFFECTIVE" TEACHING

Taylorism and Fordism were, originally, theoretical efficiency models created for engineering and factory production in the early 20th century. They were applied to education very soon after they were used to dramatically increase factory productivity. Seeking to be scientific about their work, education leaders, and the state and federal bureaucracies they interacted with to create our national school system saw both Taylorism and Fordism as useful approaches for *social* engineering of teaching and learning because they would standardize both and therefore (in theory) make them more efficient, faster, higher quality, more consistent, and more easily reproduced. It's possible and likely that the people who believed these things had good intentions. Taylorism assumes it is possible to observe a worker, identify the tasks the worker does and decisions the worker makes, and thus identify ways to eliminate repetition or duplication of tasks in mass production. Taylorism can produce false appearances that tasks and decisionmaking remain constant across time and context no matter how different the contexts are. As a result, Taylorism asserts it is not only possible but always desirable to design systems that will improve everyone's performance of a given job in the same ways at the same times to achieve the same results, every time, forever.

Similarly, Fordism as applied to schools projects corporate concepts of *effectiveness* onto education. Like Taylorism, it is based on assumptions that standardizing work will automatically increase productivity. Standardization also will require less knowledge and fewer skills from individuals, because each individual is responsible for completing only one part of the product and usually is not involved in or even aware of the full process. For example, if you go to certain fast-food restaurants that specialize in making burritos, you'll often find a standardized assembly line. One person takes your order and steams the tortilla that will deliver your delicious burrito. Another person takes that warm tortilla, but doesn't make the whole burrito. He just adds rice and your choice of beans. Another person is responsible for putting meat in your meal if you ask for it. Sometimes there are even additional people working the line who spoon in the right salsa according to your order, check the final product before wrapping it up, take your money, and hand you your meal. But the person who steamed your tortilla never sees or cares about it again once it's left his station on the line, because that's not his job.

Now, for efficiently producing burritos, that may not be a bad system. But when educating children? Not so much. Fordism is definitively a project of de-professionalizing workers and training them to follow procedures rather than make decisions to complete tasks on their own. It's an intense form of control that requires workers to *not think* because variation or deviation from the process is never acceptable. All that said, it's not hard to find symptoms of Taylorist and Fordist thinking in education. Teachers frequently get upset because students come to them without knowing things that were *supposed* to be taught in earlier grades (earlier steps in the assembly line). Many times teachers know that their students have been taught a concept before and become frustrated when they find that some still don't know it or have not achieved fluency. We blame the teacher from the grade before ours, maybe, because it was *her* job to teach it, not ours. It's important here to recognize that while that seems to make logical sense at first, we are not teaching little clones. We are teaching children, and we know from extensive research on how people learn that we can teach a group of children the exact same content at the exact same time using the exact same methods in several different places at once, and *none* of them will experience it, understand it, and learn it fluently at the same time, at the same rate, to the same level of sophistication. If that's true, it's unfair to blame our colleagues working at other stages of the process. The assumption we are making when we cast that blame is Fordist, and it might be good for making burritos but it's terrible to insist it should work in a school trying to educate young people. Applying Taylorist and Fordist ideas to public education, teaching, and learning had unintended consequences. These result from paradoxes that seem unpredictable from the perspective of rational policy decisionmaking (Bardach, 2005; Stone, 2002).

Even current reformers such as those involved with the Common Core State Standards, a set of policies created by corporate interest groups relying heavily on Taylorist and Fordist ideas, realize that classrooms and teachers should not try to operate using those factory models (National Governors Association Center for Best Practices, Council of Chief State School Officers, 2010). In their introductions to the standards for teaching and learning English language arts and mathematics, the authors state that the standards are not a curriculum and only define requirements for *basic* college and career readiness. The standards represent learning outcomes for each grade level and emphasize that teachers *must* be "free to provide students with whatever tools and knowledge their professional judgment and experience identify as most helpful" (para. 4). The standards "do not—indeed, cannot—enumerate all or even most of the content that students should learn" (para. 15). Finally, the authors of the Common Core rightly state that *no* set of standards "can fully reflect the great variety in abilities, needs, learning rates, and achievement levels of students in any given classroom" (para. 18). These clarifications are essential. We agree that having a reasonable set of standards about content to guide teachers' work can be worthwhile. But we also agree that standards are not and never will be sufficient, because teaching and learning in schools are too complicated to standardize. It's good to have clear goals as educators, and certainly we must try to be as effective in attaining those goals as possible. Well-made and well-used standards can help.

Still, the phrases "effective teaching" and "effective teachers" have become startlingly difficult problems. Denotatively, the term *effective* is defined as having a predictable result, and the U.S. education system uses it on a consistent basis along with its antonym, *ineffective*. Such labels are consistent with Taylorist/Fordist roots. However, it is widely understood that teaching, learning, human development, and the nature of schools are rarely predictable. Regardless of teacher quality, scientific findings document that both teaching and learning processes are extremely variable. Effectiveness is not the actual goal of a healthy education system. Rather, we think *effec-*

*tive* is a word that has become an inaccurate substitute for what we really want to be as teachers: *successful*. The word *successful* denotes attaining a goal regardless of method, and it means something very different from *predictable* (Burns, 2014). Where reformers talk about becoming effective, they miss their intended goal of being successful because predictability is impossible in the constantly changing contexts of our classrooms. One size does *not* fit all. And that's okay. There's a better way that we call *responsive teaching*.

## TEACHING ON PURPOSE:
## RESPONSIVE TEACHING AS A DESIGN FOR SCHOOL SUCCESS

Teaching English in the United States has been an explicit project of *acculturation* throughout most of its history. For example, as recently as 1996 the National Council of Teachers of English asserted that teachers are obligated to "monitor their instruction . . . while helping all students achieve academic success through acculturation" (p. 15). *Acculturation* denotes the imposition of cultural changes on groups or individuals who are different by substituting their traits with those from the dominant groups in a society. If we take the idea that our nation is (or ought to be) the freest in the world and the best society specifically because its citizens are diverse enough to make the society stronger, then acculturation does not sound like a wise or honest method for remaining a land of freedom. Acculturation ensures that the only way a person can achieve his dreams is to sacrifice who he actually is if he's not already like the dominant group. It raises the question of whether we are responding to students in ways that enable them to pursue their dreams, or whether we in fact are teaching them to become copies of us and pursue our dreams even if our dreams don't make sense for their futures.

Given all this, teachers need to ask what constitutes a principled, systematic approach to teaching that *does* honor our nation's diversity as the strength it is. This is more than just a moral and ethical argument. A long history of scientific experiments (Steele, 2011) has proven that when individuals are enabled to perform in environments that acknowledge, value, respect, and use their identities to help them, they almost always succeed at significantly higher levels. By the same token, when we use one-size-fits-all curriculum, instruction, and assessments that ignore difference, identity, and diversity, our students almost always perform worse.

### Responsive Teaching and Students' Funds of Knowledge

To teach on purpose, we recommend teachers link classroom study to students' *funds of knowledge*, a term originated by Moll, Amanti, Neff, and Gonzalez (1992) to describe what students bring to school with them from their everyday lives (Burns & Miller, in press; Hall, Burns, & Edwards, 2010). According to Moje et al. (2004), funds of knowledge is a fancy phrase used to describe the sources of knowledge, experience, information, and understanding that people bring with them to any new experience. These "funds" are the prior knowledge central for use in constructivist approaches to education (Dewey, 1938). Funds of knowledge also can be considered as knowledge and fluency in relation to nonacademic but school-related topics. For example, students bring knowledge with them to school about how to interact with authority figures (and how authority figures are supposed to interact with them) based on their family and community lives. Their knowledge and assumptions about this aspect of social life constitute a fund they draw on to understand and participate in new situations. Teachers can and ought to identify that knowledge as data for instructional use, analyze them, and then use them in classroom and instructional designs to support all students' abilities to fully engage and participate.

By using students' nonacademic knowledge as a legitimate centerpiece for academic study, teachers reduce what students have to know in order to participate, and also reduce the cognitive energy learners otherwise would have to spend just figuring out how to behave in a certain situation. Teachers can select texts that focus on culturally and socially relevant topics that students relate to with greater ease. By using relevant topics and resources to teach academic subjects, we empower students to engage at much higher levels. Ultimately, by reducing the amount of new information students require and making valued use of what students already know and do, responsive teaching practices like Third Space approaches (Gutierrez, 2008) reduce students' cognitive loads so they can concentrate on learning what we actually are trying to teach. Without responsive teaching, the same students spend huge amounts of cognitive energy in ways that have little or nothing to do with learning. Instead of focusing on how to read and write, students are left wasting their brains and time figuring out how to respond to teachers and peers who are not like them, how to respond to teachers' questions in ways the teacher recognizes as appropriate, how to make sense of the worksheets and directions we give them for completing assignments, and how to engage with texts and learning resources that are literally foreign to their identities and experiences.

With responsive teaching, classroom instruction and assessment are designed to reflect knowledge, practices, and literacies in contemporary society. Traditional practices are no longer sufficient. Recognition and representation of students' identities, prior knowledge, and personal experiences as different and therefore *valuable* to everyone bolster students' efficacy as learners and members of their learning community. That encourages them to develop *academic resilience*—"a disposition to focus on learning when the going gets tough, to quickly recover from setbacks, and to adapt" (Johnston & Costello, 2005, p. 257). When responsive teachers help learners practice via tasks and texts they find responsive to their identities, they are far more likely to perform successfully than they would in traditional academic contexts where their identities and knowledge are treated as coincidental.

By documenting students' knowledge and skills and *using* those data to help them see how their own experiences connect with academic knowledge, responsive teachers can take purposeful steps to position formerly marginalized students as primary knowers who *all* have perspectives, knowledge, and experiences they can use to help everyone in class learn better (Aukerman, 2007). This is responsive teaching.

### Why Responsive Teaching Matters

By asking students about their family structures, relationships, working lives, domestic activities, and household routines or traditions, teachers gain data about students' funds of knowledge as areas of skill and interest, vocabularies, and norms for social interaction. Similarly, asking students about their neighborhoods and communities provides data about students' languages, expectations, and understandings of social interaction, patterns of activity, consumer knowledge and values, communication styles, and even schedules (Moll & Gonzalez, 2001). Teachers can then use those data responsively to select texts, adapt instructional techniques to local groups, and teach in socially just ways by using scenarios students are more likely to see as useful, more likely to find valuable, and more likely to understand and use so they can fully engage during class and beyond.

Assessing and using students' funds of knowledge to contextualize teaching and classroom study leads to the kinds of engaged learning we know correlates with increased academic achievement, improved motivation, and lifelong learning (Guthrie & Wigfield, 2000). That includes improved performance related to standards and standardized assessments (Guthrie, 2002). The key to success is to blend traditional academic data with data from students' funds of knowledge to generate balanced and more responsive curriculum and instruction.

By collecting systematic data about students and groups in their classrooms, teachers can integrate new understandings in their instructional plans and classroom routines. As Risko and Walker-Dalhouse (2007) recommend, teachers can integrate students' funds into formal instruction by identifying the content to teach (topics), problems embedded in that content (opportunities for higher-order thinking), essential disciplinary content students should learn as a result of instruction (skills and concepts), and finally students' prior knowledge, "including patterns of language used in their community, at home, and with peers" (p. 99).

Even as we encourage teachers to help students via systematic assessment of their funds of knowledge, we realize current demands for accountability make it hard to implement that approach as much as they might like.

But as Marsh (2006) notes, if we don't make ourselves aware of students' identities beyond our classrooms, eventually we will all teach in ways that are "anachronistic and inadequate" (p. 173). If teachers simplistically implement the curriculum and tests required by schools and states without regard for students' existing knowledge, values, and practices, we will fail and contribute to a situation in which many students struggle not because they are unable but because we don't give them the necessary time, best possible resources, good reasons, or even the minimal opportunities they need to practice and succeed (Scherff & Piazza, 2008). Instead, we (intentionally or not) will force our students to figure out how to meet our expectations on their own when *we* should be responding to *them* in order to help them focus on what they need to learn.

Why does all this matter? Alvermann (2005) found that "the level of student engagement (including its sustainability over time) is *the* mediating factor, or avenue, through which classroom instruction influences student outcomes" (p. 196, emphasis added). Reed, Shallert, Beth, and Woodruff (2004) also found that curricula and environments that support even minimally responsive teaching positively affect students' motivations to engage with academic tasks.

By studying relationships between young peoples' identities and school engagement, some research has focused on the roles of gender in literacy learning. Studying how masculinity constructs and is constructed by texts in early adolescence, Young (2000) described how responding to male teens' identities increased their awareness of their gender identities and how those identities affected the ways they interpreted texts they studied in school—a great exercise in critical thinking and self-reflection. Chandler-Olcott and Mahar (2003b) found that supporting female students' uses of computer technology increased their engagement and motivation to read, write, and learn in school when they otherwise would not. Grisham and Wolsey (2006) found that using online formats students were familiar with to discuss literary texts increased student engagement with school, while Kim and Kamil (2004) found that students who were provided access to instruction using digital tools demonstrated increased motivation due to its relevance in their day-to-day lives.

Other research has focused on using teens' popular cultures as bridges to academic learning. Weinstein (2007) documented how the use of pop culture texts has academic value, Chandler-Olcott and Mahar (2003a) described how "fanfiction" based on students' interests in Japanese *anime* increased academic engagement, and McGinnis (2007) found that integrating youths' multilingual, multicultural, and multimodal interests and knowledge outside of school, especially those related to popular cultures, enabled teachers to create resources for learning that students found valuable.

Other studies have led to the conclusion that, as Graves (2004) has said, engagement is the "sine qua non" of literacy learning (p. 447)—the thing that successful teaching cannot do without. Alvermann et al. (1996) found that youth engaged more and saw schoolwork as more beneficial when tasks, topics, and purposes were designed by responsive teachers to be relevant to students' lives. Other scholarship reflects similar findings (e.g., Greenleaf & Schoenbach, 2001; Guthrie & Davis, 2003). These scientific studies from psychology, curriculum studies, pedagogical theory, identity theory, literacy, and other fields highlight that responding to youths' daily lives during academic study is crucial to classroom success.

## CONCLUSION

None of this is anything new or especially remarkable. It's not so much sliced bread, or a better mousetrap. Responsive teaching shouldn't be a revolutionary idea. It should be a *fundamental* idea. It's a reminder that we've known how to teach quite well for a very long time. Unfortunately, leaders in our public education system have never truly invested enough or thoroughly enough to make it work purposefully and sustain meaningful teaching and learning. Nearly a century ago, John Dewey was already explaining the basic tenets of education, and the decades that followed have resulted in countless studies supporting responsive teaching as among the most vital and successful ways of teaching young people.

In *Experience and Education* (1938), Dewey explained that healthy growth—educative growth—from any experience must be designed using variable but purposefully chosen data points, goals, and rationales that are entirely about creating environments where people of all abilities can learn well together under the guidance of a responsive teacher. According to Dewey's constructivist framework, responsive teachers (1) systematically collect data about students' prior knowledge and experiences, (2) assess those students' motivations, impulses, and desires, and then (3) initiate appropriate levels of social control in carefully designed environments in which the students are active participants who learn academic content in sincere and meaningful ways that matter to them. We believe that in addition to Dewey's methods, teachers can accomplish all of this in ways that meet any reasonable set of standards, whether they are the Common Core State Standards in widespread use today or whatever new standards may replace them. But rather than simplistically preparing students for college and career, responsive teaching also helps students become fully functioning members of society, capable citizens, and decent human beings who will continue to learn and make the world a better place for all.

As Dewey wrote, "The great waste in the school comes from [the child's] inability to utilize the experiences he gets outside of the school in any complete and free way within the school itself; while on the other hand, he is unable to apply in daily life what he is learning in school" (cited in

Street, 2003, p. 83). Responsive teaching matters because it's more than a nice thing to do. It's not just a warm and fuzzy approach to teaching, although joyful hugs in classrooms matter a lot more than most people want to admit. Responsive teaching matters because it has been proven that responding to students' identities helps them succeed (Steele, 2011). It's not just a moral argument. It never really was. It is a professional approach to teaching that understands that the impulse to learn begins with what the students desire and what they already know. Our job as teachers is to collect that information as legitimate data, analyze it, and figure out how to use every bit of it in as many ways as possible to lighten the students' cognitive loads, highlight questions that matter, and make students want to learn the content we teach. If teachers do these things, then schools, students, and the communities they live in are far likelier to grow strong and healthy. Scientific research has shown that, at the very least, our students will be more motivated to learn and engage in school and thus will do better academically. At best? They will succeed in life beyond our wildest expectations.

Responsive teaching matters. We should do it on purpose.

# CHAPTER 3

# Motivation, Engagement, and Designing Classrooms for Responsive Teaching

I've come to a frightening conclusion that I am the decisive element in the classroom. It's my personal approach that creates the climate. It's my daily mood that makes the weather. As a teacher, I possess a tremendous power to make a child's life miserable or joyous. I can be a tool of torture or an instrument of inspiration. I can humiliate or heal. In all situations, it is my response that decides whether a crisis will be escalated or de-escalated and a child humanized or dehumanized.

—Haim Ginott

### LET'S GET ENGAGED!

It doesn't take a genius to realize many young people would rather do anything than sit in school all day, 9 months per year, for 13 years. Short of putting them in a rubber room and forcing them to watch *Golden Girls* reruns *Clockwork Orange*–style, many adolescents today would choose anything except sitting through classes chosen for them because adults who don't know them have decided those classes are important for them, whether the students know it and like it or not. And, again, let's be honest: Anyone who's sat through 7–8 hours of highly routine, tightly scheduled classes every weekday for 12–13 years has felt the urge to pull a Ferris Bueller, grab a friend, and escape in a borrowed Ferrari.

And in cases where classrooms are designed so students sit in rows, don't move, rarely interact, receive commands from the teacher, and have little choice about what they do, when, or how? Such traditional modes of school are, frankly, worse than boring for anyone. They actually can teach students to view learning as undesirable. Such classes are miseducative (Dewey, 1938). That is, they impose experiences that discourage students from engaging and learning to desire more new experiences. In this chapter, we talk about how to create responsive classrooms and act in ways that make students want to learn. We'll also look at research you can use to create a learning environment for your students proven to correlate almost perfectly with increased student achievement and motivation.

Whole books have been written about how and why schools are built in ways that ironically harm our abilities to teach and learn. Phillip Jackson's *Life in Classrooms* (1990) used his research to document how, for example, rules, rituals, crowds, praise, and power all affect how teachers and students often come into conflict, with bad results, due to traditional school structures such as those listed here. These structures are still in place and dramatically affecting the nature of life in classrooms today. Teachers enforce most rules. Teachers preside over most daily rituals. Teachers manage the crowds students must live in, and teachers decide when, how, and whether to praise a student. Or not.

And yes—as this chapter's epigram from Haim Ginott (1993) highlights—teachers are usually the most powerful members in a classroom. We have the most authority to determine how students spend time, what topics they study, what materials they use, and what they do with it all to demonstrate mastery, basic understanding, or failure to learn. Students often fear teachers for these reasons. We are the faces and voices of authority for students, even when we are required to implement things we would not choose to use if we had the authority to refuse. But if you've ever had a 10th-grader ask you to stop "yelling" at him when you haven't even raised your voice, what you probably are hearing is that he is afraid of being perceived in any negative way by you because you literally determine his fate. That's a huge responsibility, isn't it? It's kind of terrifying when you take it seriously. We are responsible for much more of what happens in our classrooms than we would like to admit. But there are ways to make our central position as classroom designers and instructional facilitators into advantages for our students. Let's look at the science of self-efficacy, motivation, and engagement to learn how we can teach in ways that make it easier for students to succeed, without "spoon-feeding" them or "dumbing down" a single aspect of the work we do together.

When a student or group fails to engage with our teaching, it usually means we've either done something or *failed* to do something that made their level of engagement predictable. Maybe we used a text they couldn't relate to because it was totally foreign to their lives and identities. For example, no matter how elegant molecular structures may be in your opinion as a specialist in chemistry, do we really think 15-year-olds are going to see the relevance of covalent bonds in their daily lives? Maybe we didn't give them enough time to explore the topic so that they could make connections that *would* relate to their lives. Maybe we spent too much time creating "fun" activities and not enough time designing meaningful *tasks* based on sincere questions that mattered to them. Maybe we should spend more time considering how what *we* do as professionals affects how, why, when, and whether students engage in our classrooms. It's possible we spend far too much time blaming students for not responding to what we do, in ways that are totally predictable once we admit that we are dealing with middle and high school students.

It's important to acknowledge here that it is not always the teacher's fault when students do not or cannot engage in class. Sometimes even perfect lessons implemented by expert teachers fail, and sometimes those failures are due to problems beyond our control. Sometimes individuals or groups resist what we teach, no matter what, for reasons we cannot explain. Some can't engage because they lack reading skills, or because they have not had sufficient opportunities to learn basic concepts. Some have learning disabilities or emotional/behavioral disorders that make it hard for them to sustain attention. Some resist not because they are unable but because they do not value school for any number of reasons we may never know. In addition, we have to account for the fact that today's classrooms are places where teaching and learning frequently are interrupted for nonacademic reasons. We also must acknowledge that current accountability and reform policies require us to implement standardized tests defined by outside agencies that require us to design instruction in ways that limit our curriculum and prevent us from teaching in ways we know are healthier (Hall et al., 2010). Classroom teaching, especially helping young people focus, engage, and succeed, is messy work.

Still, there are scientifically proven strategies teachers can use to help make their classrooms purposeful places designed for meaningful teaching and high student engagement that relates strongly to increased learning. The key is to consider what Guthrie and Wigfield (2000) call an *engagement perspective* that guides how we design our classrooms, create conditions for optimal learning, and make our instruction relevant to the people who need it most: our students. This perspective requires us to consider three interrelated elements and the science behind them: self-efficacy, motivation, and engagement.

## SELF-EFFICACY, MOTIVATION, AND THE SCIENCE OF ENGAGEMENT

Scientific research has demonstrated a powerful, near-perfect correlation between classrooms that are systematically designed to engage learners and increased academic achievement, motivation, and desire to learn. To put the concept of correlation in plain terms, consider engagement and learning as two related variables in a math problem. If the level of the first variable (engagement) goes up, the level of the second variable goes up too. That is the definition of a positive correlation. In statistics, a perfect correlation score = +1.0 on a scale from -1.0 to +1.0. According to Guthrie and Wigfield (2000), when teachers purposely design classrooms and learning tasks with certain proven conditions in place, engagement correlates with learning at a level of +.8 out of +1.0. Given this, increased engagement may not *cause* increased learning. But when teachers respond to their students in systematically engaging ways, there is a near-perfect tendency for student learning to increase too. When we use engagement strategies on purpose, our students are more successful. That success tends to make them hungry for more.

And what's at the heart of a successful, engaging classroom? Several things, but three in particular: students who have been positioned to succeed and believe in their ability to keep succeeding; a teacher who designs environments and tasks that mindfully generate engagement; and purposeful instruction designed to be relevant based primarily on what the *students* find most valuable and useful.

### Self-Efficacy

Fundamentally, a student's motivation is related to her belief that she can succeed at a given task. This belief that "I can do it" is referred to as evidence of an individual's self-efficacy—her confidence that she will be able to achieve various goals (Wigfield, 1997). When students understand the purposes of learning tasks, and when those tasks are meaningful *to the students*, they feel more confident about their abilities to understand and participate. They become more willing to persist even when challenged by new tasks and goals. When students experience early and ongoing success because of relevance and persistence, they develop a sense of ability they can rely on and become more and more open to new and deeper learning (Oldfather & Dahl, 1994; Thomas & Oldfather, 1997).

The positive feelings success generates in learners' minds lead them to crave additional gratification by experiencing new successes. As the cliché goes, confidence breeds success, and success breeds more success, which breeds greater confidence, and so on. But confidence and success are not useful without meaning and sincerity, and that requires teachers to design learning tasks for lessons and units to not only generate early self-efficacy, but also build on it steadily so students are consistently motivated to engage as a matter of design. According to Reeve and Jang (2006), when teachers consistently design activities that support students' success by preserving and recognizing their competence, interests, preferences, values, and control, students' efficacy increases and they develop intrinsic motivations to participate and learn. Such findings emphasize how responsive teachers who seek to increase learning must carefully create environments in which they position students to feel capable and successful as early and often as possible.

### Motivation

Beyond self-efficacy, school motivation can be defined as a blend of internal and external reasons for participating in classes. Motivation may be intrinsic (e.g., personal enjoyment or interest) or extrinsic (e.g., rewards, praise, higher grades) (Otis, Grouzet, & Pelletier, 2005). Intrinsic motivations tend to lead to more and longer term success than extrinsic motivations, but extrinsic motives are not inherently bad. External motivators like rewards can temporarily enhance students' willingness to participate or even fully engage. But overuse of things like extra credit, prizes, or special privileges actually can *lower* or *prevent* students' engagement if (and more honestly, when) those external rewards are removed. Still, when teachers use external motivators purposefully, along with responsive classroom practices that generate interest and efficacy, students' motivations will increase and they will engage more over time. As Otis et al. (2005) report, when students decide a classroom learning task will benefit them, they often start regulating their own behaviors in ways that result in long-term intrinsic motivation.

Teachers can purposely generate motivation from many sources. Interest and attitude play roles (Guthrie & Alao, 1997; Schiefele, 1996; Schraw, 1997), and so does choice about both what resources they use and what purposes guide their work (Schraw, Flowerday, & Reisetter, 1998). Support from caring teachers plays a significant role, and so does positive social interaction (Wentzel, 1997). Intrinsic motivation often requires providing students with opportunities to choose what they study for enjoyment as much as learning, knowledge they view as useful in achieving *their* social goals (rather than the teacher's academic goals), and opportunities to satisfy their curiosity about topics they find interesting. Part of our job is making the content we teach interesting for all learners. That does not mean designing instruction using resources in ways we personally feel our students *should* find interesting. It means designing instruction and using resources in ways that we have professionally assessed *are* interesting to our students. That's true whether we are teaching content dating from hundreds of years ago or content that is on the cutting edge of contemporary thought in our fields. Our job is to make students not only learn it, but *want* to learn it and feel capable while doing so.

As important as it is for teachers to think about how to increase positive motivations, it's also necessary to keep in mind that many students come to class with negative motives that lead them to avoid participation before we've even had a chance to help them participate successfully. They devalue school and academics and even resist tasks they otherwise would enjoy and find useful (Guthrie, Coddington, & Wigfield, 2009), sometimes simply because those tasks are happening in school and they've learned to mistrust anything schools offer. Frequently as a result of past negative experiences in classrooms where teachers were not responsive to them as learners or people, students will fake reading and writing, bluff their way through discussions, refuse to do homework, and even misbehave on purpose so that they will be kicked out of class and prevented from having to do the work they wished to avoid. None of that is good, and we vote for something better. We vote to work systematically on designing engaging learning environments.

## Engagement

When students have sufficient motivation to learn in a purposely designed classroom environment focused on sincerely treating them as valuable partners in the process and helping them learn in ways that are meaningful to them, they become more likely to engage. Engagement can be defined as willing, focused, active participation. Engagement is characterized by purposeful use of strategies to achieve goals (Guthrie, Alao, & Rinehart, 1997; Guthrie & Wigfield, 2000). Engaged learners comprehend better and have stronger classroom outcomes than disengaged learners (Guthrie et al., 2006). The question, then, is this: How can teachers purposely generate positive motivations in classrooms that lead to fully engaged students?

Guthrie and Wigfield (2000) outline an *engagement perspective* that may be used to design classrooms and instruction and achieve these ends. We present the engagement perspective here as a cluster of six conditions and explain how teachers can use them to create environments in which all learners find and use motivations that increase their self-efficacy, help them engage positively and purposefully, and enable them to learn well.

## ENGAGEMENT: SIX CORE CONDITIONS

Generating classroom motivation and engagement involves establishing six basic conditions in your classroom. These conditions are not always typical or simple to generate and sustain, especially in schools where curriculum has been narrowed or instruction has been heavily standardized. In this era of standardization, teachers must work very purposefully to achieve truly engaging classrooms. The six conditions are:

- Establishing clear knowledge goals
- Providing choice and variety within structure
- Delivering explicit strategy instruction
- Providing real-world connections
- Supporting collaboration
- Being a caring teacher (Guthrie et al., 2006)

Next, we're going to take a look at each of these conditions, explain why they matter, and discuss how they work.

### Clear Knowledge Goals

Establishing knowledge goals provides learners with clear purposes for classroom work. Such a pedagogical move seems like common sense, but many teachers simply assign students to "read chapter 7 and complete exercises 1–5" for a class and call that the objective for the day's lesson, without providing explicit explanations about why they want students to do those things, or how doing them is relevant and meaningful to them as people (not students, *people*).

Providing knowledge goals such as "read chapters 1 through 3 *to identify the setting and point of view* used in the story" in English class gives readers clearer purposes for their work, for example. Instead of reading without a clear goal in mind, students know that they have two clear tasks: identify the setting of the story, and identify the point of view being used by the author. These may not seem like earth-shattering objectives, but they matter. To comprehend narrative writing, students must be able to understand where and when the story takes place. When the teacher explicitly alerts them to read with the goal of determining the point of view from which the story is being told, they can draw more accurate inferences or conclusions about many aspects of a text, including facts about the characters and events that drive the plot and its themes. With clear knowledge goals, teachers can guide students to analyze a manageable set of details rather than assign them to comprehend *everything* about a text all at once. In addition to literally making it easier for students to think about the concepts and practice the skills they need to learn, preparing and providing clear knowledge goals as a purposeful, explicit part of instruction helps students focus, successfully learn smaller chunks of knowledge at deeper levels, and build consistently on prior knowledge as they achieve a series of goals planned carefully to maximize their success.

### Choice and Variety

Providing a variety of interesting learning tools and resources, and allowing students some choice in both what they do and how they participate, also increases motivation and engagement (Ivey & Broaddus, 2001; Kottke, 2008). For example, adolescents often struggle with academic reading not because they can't read, but because school texts don't interest them (Allington, 2007; Lenters, 2006). When they are allowed to participate in the choices of the texts they read, the tasks they complete using those texts, or the peers they interact with while reading, their motivation increases and they become more purposefully engaged (Guthrie et al., 2006). Similarly, when students are allowed to study topics *they* find interesting (versus being forced to study topics the teacher decided they *ought* to find interesting), they become much more engaged for intrinsic reasons. Similarly, and importantly, when learners are allowed some choice in the formats and types of resources and texts they use, especially new media formats and multiple types of media at the same time, their engagement and motivation tend to increase (Botzakis & Burns, 2013; Burns & Botzakis, 2012).

Even in places where the availability of obviously relevant texts is limited, teachers can design tasks using themes and sincere questions that are meaningful to students' personal lives and values. Teachers can use these meaningful themes and questions to provide students with a range of options that can all be useful for demonstrating learning. For example, while reading Roth's *Divergent* (2011), students might be given the option to (1) compare characters from the novel, (2) script and produce a video interpreting characters' behaviors or the text's tone in a pivotal scene, or (3) design and explain a soundtrack they would use to communicate the meaning, themes, tone, and mood of the story in sequence with the plot. These alternatives provide structured choice *and* variety so teachers can maintain order even as students show their learning in a variety of ways. When students have choices, their intrinsic motivation goes up. When they don't, they disengage and/or develop negative motivations for schooling (Lenters, 2006).

## Explicit Strategy Instruction

To complement the use of clear knowledge goals, teachers also should explicitly introduce and model strategies students can practice repeatedly and at length for increased classroom success, such as predicting, summarizing, and questioning content in a text, regardless of the content area. These two conditions alone—providing clear learning goals and explicit strategy instruction—have a significant positive impact on students' learning over time. Grolnick and Ryan (1987) found that when students received clear knowledge goals for academic reading, their comprehension increased more than that of students who simply were told to do their work and try hard on tests. Spires and Donley (1998) found that explaining how learning strategies work results in greater understanding of academics and positive attitudes about learning. Focusing learners on attainable goals and showing them how to use strategies to attain those goals helps them experience success sooner and more often. As a result, doing so improves their self-efficacy and increases their motivations to engage more and more.

## Real-World Interactions

In addition to clear goals, choices and variety, and strategy instruction, teachers can generate real-world interactions to increase engagement. A real-world experience might entail taking the opportunity to listen to and interview a Holocaust survivor in social studies class, while reading Anne Frank's *The Diary of a Young Girl* (1993). Or it might consist of simulating the terrifying setting described in Poe's short story "The Pit and the Pendulum" (1983) to consider concepts like mood, tone, and symbolism. It is not that students actually, physically must experience the situations, concepts, and ideas they study. Rather, they benefit immensely from purposely designed, multiple opportunities to get involved with the texts they read and to use the concepts and skills they learn instead of passively listening while their teachers tell them what those texts and concepts mean and how they *might* be used. Journaling, active questioning techniques, guest speakers and fieldtrips, creative drama activities, experiments, simulations, and mock debates all entail real events, authentic interactions, and purposeful experiences that stimulate students' thinking in ways that increase positive motives for learning.

### Collaboration

One of the reasons why real-world interactions increase classroom engagement is that they require students to interact. According to Guthrie and Davis (2003), collaboration requires students to depend on one another as they work to achieve goals. Collaborative activities also can be designed so students are given explicit opportunities to participate in the norms of their classroom. For example, during learning tasks, teachers can coach students to practice using terms and applying concepts needed for successful learning in a content area. Doing so enables students to talk with one another in ways that are both academically meaningful and personal, while still remaining fun. While ideally collaborative tasks may be enjoyed by all learners, the actual point of collaboration is to help teachers provide students with opportunities to not only learn concepts and skills, but also use them in real ways with other people. By providing repeated opportunities to hear and apply disciplinary terms and concepts in collaborative groups during math class, for example, teachers help students retain knowledge in ways that are proven to significantly increase academic success (Marzano, Pickering, & Pollock, 2001).

### A Caring Teacher

Students' motivation in any classroom increases when they believe their teacher cares for and understands them as individuals. In fact, research about "teacher expectations" (e.g., Nash, 2012) demonstrates repeatedly that when teachers think, plan, and act with the purposeful expectation that all students are capable of succeeding at a given learning task, their students are significantly more likely to succeed. The phenomenon has been documented so often that it earned its own name: the Pygmalion effect (Rosenthal, 2002). Related to self-efficacy, when teachers purposefully treat their students like capable participants and successful learners on a consistent basis, those students tend to behave in ways that generate self-fulfilling prophecies. The teacher designs the classroom and all instruction based on the fundamental belief that students can and will succeed as a direct result of that design and their own abilities to learn with the teacher's guidance. The students, based on the teacher's purposefully designed instructional materials, succeed early and often in legitimate ways that increase their belief that they are capable. Over time, students working with such a caring teacher will begin to behave in ways that directly contribute to and manifest success.

According to Klem and Connell (2004), adolescent students are three times as likely to report being engaged when they feel their teachers care. When teachers overtly demonstrate warmth and encouragement, students feel more comfortable, welcomed, capable, and motivated to try (Skinner & Belmont, 1993). Displaying warmth does not mean a teacher shouldn't challenge students, or that she shouldn't push them to work hard, or that she would be wise to dumb down the curriculum early and often so students get a free ride that lends the illusion of success. It means the teacher must consciously show all students that they can succeed, and that the teacher is working very clearly to support that success all the way.

The six conditions described above create an engagement perspective that teachers can use to make their work and their students more successful, more positive, and more meaningful.

## "BECAUSE I SAID SO":
## ENGAGEMENT AND THE PROBLEM OF TEACHER BIAS

On top of the pure logistical chaos of managing classrooms full of young people who don't always want to be there, teachers bring their own motives to the show. Because that's undeniably true, we acknowledge that creating and sustaining an engaging environment is a lot harder than we usually want to believe. According to Lortie (1975), teachers' motives commonly include a desire to share and continue their own enthusiastic study of topics they enjoyed when they were students themselves. We tend to teach as we were taught, and we tend to believe that the ways in which we learned best are the ways everyone else learns and likes best too. Our motives in this regard have consequences, mostly negative. As Dewey (1944) wrote, teaching today's students as we were taught yesterday prevents them from learning what they need to learn for tomorrow.

Teachers, we hope, have significant passion, enthusiasm, and regard for the subjects they teach. These can be and often are powerful tools for engagement when used strategically. But when we are not purposeful about using that passion, it can lead to unfortunate consequences. In loving our subjects, we sometimes assume everyone else will (or ought to) love them just as much as we do. If only they would try, we just know they finally would understand and develop the same love of learning we have! When teachers fall into this trap, we have a bad habit of assuming that what our students should think and how they ought to behave are mostly a matter of common sense and following instructions. Sometimes we assume those activities and behaviors are so obvious that we don't even name them, let alone teach our students about them. Even when such expectations *are* communicated to students, they often come in the form of rules and rituals organized according to the needs of the school or the teacher more than the needs of the students. We do certain things in school because they are the ways school has always been done, even when we cannot explain why, or even when those methods don't help students or directly lead to their failure (Tyack & Cuban, 1995). Jackson (1990) famously talked about these invisible traditions of classroom life actually getting in the way of meaningful teaching. Faced with mandatory attendance and participation in activities they do not recognize as useful, interesting, or relevant, adolescent students predictably respond by going off task, acting out in boredom or frustration, failing because they have not been taught what actually is targeted for them to learn during class, or otherwise struggling to engage with us in ways we recognize as appropriate.

As teachers, our love for our own content areas creates an unfortunate habit in our work: We develop a tendency to believe we know what our students need, how and who they ought to be, and what they should do with the things they learn from us. We come to think our students *ought* to find the things we teach and do engaging because *we* happen to find them engaging for *ourselves*. When they fail to respond as enthusiastically as we do to reading about geological epochs in science class, for example, many teachers often will do anything but acknowledge that geological history might not be automatically and self-evidently relevant for today's students. After all, what teenager *wouldn't* be interested in the factors involved in the formation of the Earth's multiple layers of crust? That's something everybody finds important to know someday, right? Clearly no, because only a minority of teenagers automatically think that the ground they walk on is actually as fascinating as it really is (and it is!). We judge our students harshly in English classes when they don't find close readings of Hamlet's soliloquys to be useful. We become frustrated when they wonder in math class how something like algebra is going to be relevant in their lives. When they fail to engage in writing tasks, we threaten them with bad grades and dire warnings that they won't do well in college unless they do the work. When students complain that a topic or text is boring, we lament that they can't appreciate quality or that they lack respect. If they resist by going off task because they are bored, we label them immature. If they resist by not trying, we accuse them of being lazy.

Sometimes it's more insidious. When we spend hours setting up a lesson around a group discussion or collaborative task and the lesson falls flat, we often claim our students are *unable* to engage with such complex tasks. Most of the time—far too often—we forget to consider the obvious logical explanations for why students sometimes refuse to participate in the lessons we create. We forget that our job is to respond to *them* and help them *want* to learn what we teach, not force them to do what we say because we're their teachers and we said so.

These supposedly hidden effects of professional motives and expectations in classrooms often prevent professionals from successfully teaching students. Consideration of our own motives when teaching a subject helps us be more intentional about designing instruction that gives our students as many opportunities as possible to develop the self-efficacy and positive motives they need to engage fully and succeed at consistently high levels. Even when teachers work to make certain instructional plans have engaging "activities" in them, traditional approaches to school and teaching make it hard for young people to succeed as much as they could if we responded to them instead of forcing them to respond to us. Engagement cannot be generated or sustained by inserting some single, special activity or another to spice up the day. Classroom engagement is achieved and sustained by purposeful work and thoughtful professional designs. Engaged learning is not accidental.

## CONCLUSION

Teaching on purpose contributes to a self-sustaining pattern of motivations for both teachers and students that corresponds with lifelong learning behaviors and a persistent sense of efficacy. The earlier we experience success, the more confident we all feel. The more confident we feel about our abilities, the better we feel about ourselves and seek to do more. The more we succeed on purpose, the more we want to experience additional success together. Finally, the more often we work together on sincere issues, the more successful we tend to be. That success depends, first and foremost, on knowing who our students are and making their identities the center of our work.

# CHAPTER 4

# Using Students' Funds of Knowledge to Plan on Purpose

> Being busy does not always mean real work. The object of all work is production or accomplishment and to either of these ends there must be forethought, system, planning, intelligence, and honest purpose, as well as perspiration. Seeming to do is not doing.
>
> —Thomas Edison

## INTRODUCTION

We've mentioned the fundamental need to integrate students' own prior knowledge and day-to-day experiences as integral parts of classroom instruction several times so far in this book. Doing so enhances instruction and learning. But if your professional preparation was anything like ours, you probably were taught how to make lessons and unit plans using procedural techniques focused almost solely on academic learning, like those developed by Hunter (1982). If so, you might recall that "the Hunter model" of instructional planning has seven steps: (1) reviewing, (2) providing an "anticipatory set" (activating students' prior academic knowledge), (3) stating a single clear objective for each lesson, (4) offering input and modeling new academic content and its uses, (5) formative assessment, (6) guided student practice, and finally (7) independent student performance to evaluate mastery (summative assessment). That approach has become classic. It is consistent, coherent, and logical as a basic approach to teaching in any traditional classroom.

Other readers may have learned how to plan using approaches like the one offered in now-classic textbooks like *Understanding by Design* (Wiggins & McTighe, 2005). In that model, focused on unit-level planning, you might remember the promotion of a technique referred to as *backward design* and a process like this:

1. Identify desired standards-based academic outcomes (What should students know and be able to do with new content based on subject-area standards?).
2. Identify criteria for student understanding (What evidence is required to assess and evaluate student learning?).
3. Plan instruction to frame student experiences in class (What new information will students need in order to support new learning? How will they practice independent use of new academic knowledge and skills? What sequence of experiences and resources will be most helpful to improve their academic abilities?).

In this model, teachers are encouraged to consider desired academic results first, then to design instruction with that end in mind so all classroom activities align with that end goal (often and traditionally a summative assessment for a final grade).

Both of these models have been and remain useful and valuable for thinking about how to plan for traditional academic instruction. They are logical and offer clear procedures any professional could use to teach and assess students' academic knowledge. Still, both are missing important elements. Neither approach focuses attention on the central role of students' identities and experiences. While Wiggins and McTighe focus considerably (and usefully) on generating questions that provide learners with *academically* relevant topics, their discussions of how and why to use questions, along with other instructional elements, do not address the aspect of our work we know is crucial to success: knowing, understanding, and responding to our students.

McTighe and Wiggins (2013) explain that well-designed questions meet the following criteria: They engage students in inquiry, enable multiple possible answers, provoke additional questions, encourage discussion, require evidence, frame "big ideas" or "pressing issues," recur over time, and deepen students' understanding of a topic (Wiggins & Wilbur, 2015, para. 3). All this is desirable. Unfortunately, all of it also presumes teachers already and always know everything we need to know about what is best for all our students. They offer us mostly prescriptive steps they say will result in strong questions to drive instruction for any group of students, anywhere, anytime, all the time. They assume teaching is purposeful *enough* as long as we represent academic knowledge in logical ways. Finally, they assume the fundamental key to success is to focus on transmitting academic knowledge to students for (mostly) academic application.

Procedural approaches like those described here fail to adequately account for (or even assess) what students *actually* find purposeful and *actually* see as big ideas important to their lives, or what makes novices *actually* likely and willing to recognize a topic as relevant to life outside school. In effect, traditional approaches set aside Dewey's (1938) well-proven assertion that constructing experiences for student learning entails making plans that begin with attention to data about who our students are and how we might utilize their existing knowledge and experiences both within *and* beyond school to grow and learn.

To repeat, Dewey  famously warned that "the great waste in the [traditional] school comes from [the child's] inability to utilize the experiences he gets outside of the school in any complete and free way within the school itself; while on the other hand, he is unable to apply in daily life what he is learning in school" (pp. 77–78, cited in Street, 2003, p. 83). As a result, while the Hunter model and backward planning can be useful for planning *procedures*, they aren't enough if teachers seek to operate as truly responsive educators.

## TEACHERS KNOW BEST?
## A CAUTIONARY TALE ABOUT WALKING IN OTHERS' FOOTSTEPS

Traditional (and still active) planning approaches are symptomatic of a problem many teachers have. If we're honest, we have a longstanding bad habit of presuming we know what our students already know, and what they *should* already know and be able to do when they enter our classes. Perhaps among our greatest sins as teachers is deciding what our students *ought* to find interesting, valuable, and relevant in the content we teach, and what they *should* find purposeful. We know from personal experience that educators approach planning this way all the time. *And it isn't good enough.*

Systematic, logical planning for transmission of academic content is absolutely a primary aspect of our work. Logical procedures for structuring plans are necessary but not sufficient. Here's one example of how and why approaches to purposeful teaching often don't work because we fail to consider *who* we actually are teaching and what they really need in order to succeed, focusing instead on what *we* think should be valued. It comes from Les's experience as a teacher in the 1990s, when he decided a song about dinosaurs would get his students really engaged in studying metaphors.

## THE ROAD (THAT SHOULD NOT BE) TAKEN

Les was a 10th-grade English teacher in 1999, and he needed to teach the concept of metaphor to his students in rural Kansas. How? He didn't want to throw Dead White Guy poetry at hormonally explosive 15-year-olds. He wanted them to get a taste of what classic literature could be like, sure. But he also figured they would find class more interesting if they had the chance to learn about metaphor from poetry that wasn't older than their great-grandparents. Like countless other English teachers who also couldn't dance, he figured using some awesome pop music about a modern social issue would help students realize that poetry is totally cool.

Les chose a song by the band The Police, which some readers may remember was a popular band that included now-adult-contemporary artist Sting as its lead singer and bass player. Others are now looking up Sting on Wikipedia to figure out who the heck would think it's okay to rename himself "Sting" just because his actual name was "Gordon." But what was this awesome, can't-miss song that would drive kids to poetic ecstasy? "Walking in Your Footsteps," an atmospheric song in which the lyrics are an extended metaphor equating humans with dinosaurs, and referring to the idea that people could become extinct as the result of nuclear war. It had guitars, it had Sting. It had dinosaurs. It had nuclear war in it somewhere. So far, so good, so he thought. It was a popular song from a popular record by a popular rock band, it was entirely a metaphor, and it was about a big idea. What could possibly go wrong?

Les planned using both the Hunter model *and* backward planning. All the parts were in place. There were many ways to answer the questions: "Are humans as smart as we think we are?" "What can we learn about people by comparing ourselves to other things?" and "How can we use figurative language to explain how our world works?" Les thought these were good questions. They met all the criteria; he planned with an outcome in mind and worked backward to make sure activities would support the use of metaphors, and he structured his lesson to review with his students, activate their prior knowledge, explain new content, and then model its use. And it really did seem like a good idea at the time, if by "at the time" you meant the early 1980s rather than the late 1990s.

Before he could get to the part where students would practice and he could check for understanding, the lesson was dead. Why? It was doomed because Les never stopped to consider what his students *actually* would think of as "cool"—let alone valuable or relevant. And they didn't think it was cool. At all.

The students had no idea a band called The Police ever existed. That band broke up in 1983, about the time they were born, and didn't exist in their lives. In desperation, Les mentioned this was the band that gave the world Sting. (The world can be cruel sometimes.) That guy had a bunch of hit records, remember? No. They did not remember. The students responded not just by asking, "Sting who?" They also (and with good reason) asked Mr. Burns, "What's a 'record'?" These were reasonable responses because (1) Sting was not familiar to most teenagers in the late 1990s, and (2) by 1999 most students had no idea a "record" was a piece of pressed vinyl on which music was inscribed. They used their own now-obsolete technology to play music—the then-revolutionary compact disc. "Records" were things their grandparents kept in attic boxes.

Beyond simply being far out of his students' actual pop culture milieu, the topics and text Les picked were major flops for engaging his students' lives: The Cold War ended 10 years before the lesson, when his students were 5 years old and thought a "cold war" meant having a snowball fight. A song about nuclear war by an old British guy was never a wise choice. It was only meaningful to Les. It was meaningful to the teacher. And it failed.

Les fell victim to the teacher's equivalent of getting involved in a land war in Asia. He presumed he already knew what his students would find interesting. He assumed if he picked a "modern" song, it would be something they *should* and *would* find relevant, cool, useful, and purposeful. The problem was that the criteria he used were essential in those ways only to *him*. His students could not have cared less, and based on his assumptions the lesson failed. The students couldn't make sense of the poem's context. They didn't relate to the topic. And there was nothing in the lesson they felt merited attention because it was too outdated to be relevant in their lives.

Les is not the only teacher to fall victim to his own biases (and it wouldn't be the last time). Many readers are no doubt thinking about their own greatest failed attempts to be "the cool teacher." That said, these incidents result from our bad habit of assuming purposefulness, and our false assumptions have dangerous consequences (see Dewey's quote above). Too often, what teachers presume students need, find purposeful, and view as relevant enough to engage with is based on the *teachers'* personal preferences (or what they enjoyed when they were students themselves). But we are not our students. Times change, and therefore relevance and purpose are rarely stable. They are always-evolving concepts that depend on us, if we want to succeed, paying responsive attention to what our students *actually* know, value, and do in their lives.

If we want to be responsive teachers, then technical procedures for planning instruction are important but not enough. They must include *both* logical structure *and* the fullest use possible of what our students already know, do, value, and use. The content of planning should be as contemporary as possible, where contemporary means *of and with the times*. Without that attention to positioning our students at the center of our plans, we cannot genuinely engage them. They require multiple opportunities to learn and practice using new concepts and skills, and require alternatives to use their learning in their own lives for their own reasons and purposes, depending on what *they* perceive as useful and relevant beyond mere academic study. That's not to say we shouldn't teach academic content. We must. But *how* and *why* matter, and having the technical parts in place is only the beginning of teaching on purpose.

## RESPONSIVE TEACHING IN INSTRUCTIONAL DESIGN

In our experiences as teachers and teacher educators, we've seen all kinds of unit plans and lessons. No doubt you have too. At one end of the range are broad outlines based on a topic word or phrase, followed by a list of activities that might or might not be connected to particular specific content-area standards. That version of a plan might be familiar to readers as "outlining" and looks something like Figure 4.1.

While altered significantly, it is important for readers to know the plan presented in Figure 4.1 was drawn from an actual plan used by actual teachers in an actual public high school, and actual students were expected to learn how argumentation works by using it. *And it is not good enough.* It is not responsive to students, and it is not designed to be. It lacks even the most basic procedural components discussed early in this chapter as key elements of any instructional plan. We question whether the teachers, let alone their students, could make sense of such a plan's intended content, procedural requirements, or outcomes, except that the topic apparently was written argumentation and that instruction would involve heavy doses of textbook reading, quizzes, and reviews of individual rhetorical techniques traditionally used in academic writing.

We've seen units like this designed and implemented, as well as lessons that had minute-by-minute instructions for when and how to move during a lab task in chemistry, and even what exactly to say when modeling how to use primary source texts in social studies classes. Some teachers seem to believe they can succeed using nothing more than a few basic notes, while others prefer and even require whole scripts and specified instructions to control the lesson every second. Most planning falls somewhere in between, mostly due to the "triage" mode of teaching described in Chapter 1. When we operate only in terms of triage, we simply cannot be as purposeful as we must be if we want to attain real student success and do more than "get through" our lessons to "cover" the content. That isn't good enough either.

We don't pretend the basic planning components we will discuss in this and future chapters are revolutionary. As noted, the Hunter model and backward planning approaches described earlier are now traditional for good reasons. They enable basic planning for academic instruction. Chances are nearly every reader with any teaching experience is familiar with some if not all of the basic instructional elements that follow, from context descriptions to learning targets to procedural steps to assessments to standards alignment.

Most teachers use the basic components we will explain here as organizational guides to ensure their plans flow logically and cover content—whether that means following a textbook on a schedule or arranging classroom activities so students will be more likely to receive all the information about disciplinary concepts and skills they need in order to be assessed during class. Many readers, no doubt, plan in more sophisticated ways. That said, we

**Figure 4.1. A Plan Without a Purpose**

Day 1: Intro to the class

1. Syllabus
2. Turn in summer project
3. Pass out Argumentation handout and chapter 1 of textbook
4. Bias
5. Homework: Read chapter 1

Day 2:

1. Chapter 1 quiz
2. Ethos, Pathos, Logos
3. Credibility
4. Formative Assessment: Have students practice identifying ethos, pathos, and logos in their own research
5. Homework: Read chapter 12

Day 3:

1. Chapter 12 quiz
2. Lesson: Review chapter 12 and introduce defining main ideas
3. Reading rhetorically and having conversations with a text
4. Read a piece to analyze how the author establishes a main idea
5. Formative Assessment: Swift's "A Modest Proposal"
6. Lab during second half of class to find/replace sources
7. Read chapter 4 (logical appeals)

Day 4:

1. Chapter 4 quiz
2. Lesson: Review logical appeals and discuss how to select arguments and use when writing a research paper
3. Introduce position paper and annotated bibliography assignments
4. Developing a research question and writing initial thesis statements
5. Formative Assessment: Turn in research question and thesis statement
6. Homework: Read chapter 5 (ethical appeals)

Etc.

1. [The format and style of the above content continues through a 15-lesson planned writing process in which students produce an argumentative essay that serves as the summative assessment for the unit.]

recommend a particular approach to design and planning, which we consider as central to our work as teachers across all subject areas if our goal is to respond to all students and help *them* succeed.

Based on what we know from Chapters 2 and 3 about responsive teaching and the psychologies of engaging students in their own learning, we recommend teachers think about engagement as the sine qua non or "that with which we cannot do without" of learning (Graves, 2004). If we accept that as a first principle, it means placing students' identities and knowledge at the center of our instructional design work, then using what we systematically learn about their identities and knowledge as *data* to design learning tasks and sequence them in ways that help us respond during class. It provides structure to guide students and ourselves, and generates intentional environments where everyone has consistently meaningful tasks for learning the concepts and practicing the skills they need to succeed.

## BEYOND PROCEDURES: PLANNING FOR
## ENGAGED LEARNING AND RESPONSIVE TEACHING

Unlike most discussions of instructional planning, which focus on particular components and the procedural steps required to plan, we argue that professionals must be capable of not only naming and using those planning steps but also explaining *how* and *why* as professionals they operate in a given context alter, vary, or change plans when teaching another group or working in a different context. That ability to explain *how* and *why* is the heart of purposeful teaching, and purposeful teaching is the hallmark of a true professional.

Thus, the bedrock of successful teaching is purposefully designed planning for content-area instruction that is responsive to student identities. That means the first thing we have to consider before designing any plan is the data we have about who our students are, what they know, and how to use that knowledge to bridge their day-to-day experiences beyond school into our classrooms. Doing so very literally lightens their cognitive load (the amount of actual brainpower they must use to make sense of an experience and participate successfully). It also enables us to generate instruction that is more consistently engaging for more (if not all) students.

To review and expand on our definition of engagement from Chapter 3, *engaged learning* entails designing for and producing active student participation in learning tasks and content-area practices for students' own purposes in ways that are relevant to *them* as independent agents in their own lives (Hruby et al., in press). Engaged learning is an outcome of teachers' instructional designs in which students learn concepts, practice skills needed to apply them, and use that learning to do things that meet their goals and empower them to create new meanings for their future use. How do professionals purposefully design instruction for this kind of engagement? We recommend using what are referred to as "funds of knowledge" (e.g., Moll & Gonzalez, 2001).

## PLANNING FOR ENGAGED LEARNING
## USING STUDENTS' FUNDS OF KNOWLEDGE

By understanding and using students' prior knowledge and experiences out-side of school as data to design instruction for classrooms, teachers can and should develop plans at the unit and lesson levels that bridge in-school and out-of-school student learning by creating a kind of "Third Space" (Gutiérrez, 2008). A Third Space approach to teaching combines in- and out-of-school learning and experiences so classrooms become collaborative environments where participants use what they already know and do every day to learn new academic content and practices, new practical skills, and more sophisticated uses of concepts than they understood about the world and how things work (Gutiérrez, 2008; Moje, 2008). Moll et al. (1992) and Moje et al. (2004) have offered categories for different types of knowledge ("funds") that all learners always bring with them to school. The goal is to think about how educators can use those data to design instruction that responds to students' identities in ways that help them succeed in any aca-demic program.

Students' funds of knowledge (FoK) come from many contexts. In this section we offer a question protocol for collecting data about the knowledge, skills, interests, activities, and texts students engage with during their every-day lives beyond school. Our categories and questions are research-based and address five basic areas:

- Home and family funds
- Community funds
- Popular culture funds
- Personal activity funds
- General knowledge funds (e.g., Friese, Alvermann, Parkes, & Rezak, 2008; Ivey & Broaddus, 2001; Moje et al., 2004; Moll et al., 1992; Risko & Walker-Dalhouse, 2007)

Our categories are meant as models for professionals to adapt based on the needs of students in their content areas. The categories are *not* a prescriptive list to ask all students everywhere in exactly the same ways, and definitely not all at once. Teachers should strategically select categories and adapt questions depending on who their students are, what they are teach-ing, and which questions will be useful.

It is essential to emphasize that no single professional or group of teach-ers has the time to collect every bit of FoK data they might about every student. Rather, our approach enables teachers (and certainly groups at the departmental or school level) to collect data by simply observing and talking with students in their classrooms, asking them to respond to questions from useful FoK categories that reveal their orientations for studying a given subject, and finally considering whether and how to use those data for plans that are more likely to engage as many students as possible. Teachers in any content area can collect useful data about their students' funds by having students journal in response to FoK questions or write a few sentences in response to bell-ringer tasks or exit slip assessments, and even during central academic discussions and class presentations. Collecting FoK data doesn't require much work beyond what teachers are already doing with students. It makes that work more purposeful.

As noted in Chapter 3, instruction founded on student engagement correlates almost perfectly with increased motivation, persistence, learning, and achievement. It is not at all a casual matter of asking questions merely to build relationships with students (although it will support that aspect of teachers' work too). The questions can be asked and discussed during class through conversation as teachers demonstrate overt interest in their students' lives, which in itself increases student engagement levels. But teachers can go further and explain to their students that they are interested to know these things not just because they care, but because what students tell them helps them learn what students need in order to succeed. Using funds of knowledge as the foundation of instructional planning helps teachers identify, design, and frame explicit learning goals that are keys to increasing engaged learning. It also shows teachers' respect for students and their lives.

## COLLECTING STUDENTS' FUNDS OF KNOWLEDGE

We recognize that students in U.S. schools are highly diverse, even within a single classroom. Any class's collective responses to FoK questions are likely to vary. Individuals may feel uncomfortable revealing aspects of their family and home lives to teachers and peers—with good reasons. Others might be concerned about sharing personal information or intensely private cultural values that may even be taboo to share. Some simply may feel embarrassed to disclose in public what they know or don't know. We need to let students know that we respect the boundaries they choose to impose, but that knowing their funds of knowledge will help us teach them better and allow them to use what they know to learn better. We also realize some students can be overly eager and respond far beyond the intentions of data collection for planning. We encourage teachers to be explicit about the purposes of FoK data collection: to learn who students are as individuals, understand where they come from, and *use* what they already know and like to help them learn new things related to academics and schooling necessary for adult life.

Assessing students' funds of knowledge is not about forcing them to reveal private details so we can exploit them. It's about learning who they are, what they do, and what they value so we can help them.

We also realize the list of questions offered here will never be complete or address every possible topic. Our questions and categories are in some ways arbitrary. Teachers can and should adapt them to generate the most useful data for *their* contexts and subjects. Just as important, teachers must remember that FoK data don't undercut any need to cover subject-area content. They focus the content in ways learners can understand and relate to with higher engagement.

For example, a teacher who uses students' knowledge of video games to teach algorithms in algebra is not "teaching video games" in math class and should never allow students, colleagues, administrators, or parents to think that's the case. In a funds of knowledge approach, that teacher is using *data* to identify and use topics, models, and resources related to video games her students report knowing, using, and valuing. That teacher is using *data* to design instruction and learning tasks that will help students understand, talk about, and practice disciplinary knowledge and skills in math class. When teachers can explain to stakeholders how using students' funds increases academic success without dumbing down the curriculum, they generally will experience support and even encouragement.

Figure 4.2 presents the five categories noted above with questions teachers can use to collect data about who their students are, learn what they know, and use those data to make more responsive decisions in class.

## USING STUDENTS' FUNDS OF KNOWLEDGE

By asking students about their family lives, relationships, work, domestic activities, household routines, and traditions, teachers gain data about students' funds of knowledge as areas of skill and interest, vocabularies, and norms for social interaction. Asking about learners' neighborhoods and communities helps teachers use data about students' languages, expectations and understandings of social interaction, day-to-day activities, consumer values, communication styles, and even schedules. Asking what they know about a topic and why they learned it (or not) enables teachers to understand how and why students are likely to respond to resources and tasks used in the classroom. Purposeful professionals can then use such data to select resources, adapt methods, design tasks, and teach subject-area content and practices using scenarios students recognize, value, and participate in as engaged learners. Similarly, learning what a group of students generally knows or believes about interacting with authority figures outside of school can help teachers plan instruction using tones, styles, and language they can adapt to suit different groups and diverse individuals they work with throughout each day.

**Figure 4.2. Funds of Knowledge Categories and Student Data Questions**

Category 1: Family and Home Life Funds of Knowledge

1. Describe your family.
2. Where did your family come from? What do these origins mean to you and your family?
3. Do you have any brothers or sisters? How old are they? How would you describe your relationships with them?
4. Describe your parents.
5. Do you have other relatives you are close to? Where are they? How are they important to you?
6. What do you talk about with your family when you are together?
7. What kinds of things do you do with your family when you are together?
8. What are your roles in your family?
9. What traditions does your family have? What do these traditions mean to you?
10. What things do you believe your family values most? What do these values mean to you?
11. What kinds of chores do you and your family members do at home?
12. What kinds of work do you see your relatives doing at home? How do you help them?
13. Do you work outside of your home and school? What kinds of work do you know how to do?
14. Do your brothers and sisters work outside of home or school? If so, what do you know about the work they do?
15. What kinds of reading and writing do your family members and you do? Do members of your family read or write for pleasure and work? Do you?
16. How do you think your family has affected who you are as a person?
17. Does your family have any special goals or expectations for what you do, how you behave, or who you become? If so, how do you feel about these goals and expectations? Why?
18. What goals do you have for yourself in life?                      *(continued on next page)*

When teachers design curriculum on purpose using resources, knowledge, and experiences from students' funds of knowledge, they become able to position students as primary knowers (Aukerman, 2007)—full members of their classroom communities who have valuable knowledge and experiences to contribute and can help others learn too. Primary knowers therefore become collaborating agents in their own learning and participate more fully. Their out-of-school knowledge and identities are explicitly treated as not only positive but *valuable* and *necessary* for academic success. When students are supported this way using the *engagement perspective* described in Chapter 3, they succeed more. So do teachers.

Figure 4.2. Continued

Category 2: Community Funds

1. Where do you live? What's it like there? What's the geography like? What kinds of homes do people live in? What do you see every day?
2. How would you describe your neighborhood to someone from a different part of the world?
3. Who lives in your neighborhood? What do you know about them? How do you feel about them?
4. What do you know about the kinds of work people from your neighborhood do?
5. Name the most important or popular places in your community. What do these places mean to you?
6. What activities do you do most in your neighborhood? Why?
7. What do you think are the most important values of people overall in your neighborhood? Why?
8. What kinds of organized activities happen in your community? Are there festivals, or sports, or special events that are important? What do these mean to you?
9. In your opinion, what are the most important things you've learned from living in your community? Why are these things meaningful to you?

Category 3: Popular Culture Funds

1. What have you learned or read [about x: name of topic or class subject] recently? Why?
2. What have you learned in your life about [topic x] that was meaningful to you? Why?
3. What do you like/dislike about [topic x]? Why?
4. What's an interesting thing you know about [topic x]? Why is that interesting for you?
5. What magazines do you read? Why?
6. What are your favorite television shows of all time? Why?
7. What television shows are you watching right now? Why do you like them?
8. What are your favorite movies? Why?
9. What are the best movies you've seen lately? Why did you like them better than others?
10. If you use the Internet, what sites do you visit and use? Why?
11. What do you use the Internet for most?
12. When you have a computer, what do you use it for most?
13. Do you use social media or other kinds of apps? How often? What do you use? What do you dislike, not use, or try to avoid? Why?
14. Do you have a smartphone/cellphone? How do you use it? How often? Why?
15. What are your favorite kinds of music? What artists or groups do you like to listen to most? Why? What music are you listening to right now? Why do you like that music more than other kinds? Are there any kinds of music or performers you do not like? Why?

Figure 4.2. Continued

16. If you listen to music/talk radio, streaming media (music, podcasts, etc.), what do you listen to? Why?
17. What video games do you play? What do you like about those games? Are there games you don't like? Why?
18. What makes you want to read, watch, do, or listen to something? How do you decide? What makes you dislike an activity or topic?
19. What celebrities do you like? What makes them special for you? What celebrities do you dislike? How come?
20. How do you feel when teachers use music, TV shows, movies, and other things you enjoy outside of school to teach [topic or subject x]?

## Category 4: Personal Activity Funds

1. When you have free time, how do you spend it? Why?
2. What do you like to do for fun? Why?
3. What kinds of things do you do when you are with friends? Why?
4. What kinds of things do you enjoy doing on your own? Why?
5. What do you look for in a friend?
6. What makes you a good friend?
7. Do you have any hobbies? How did you learn about them? What do they mean to you?
8. Are you involved in any organized activities like sports, theater, dance, music, or arts/crafts? Why?
9. Do you participate in any other organized activities like youth groups, volunteer organizations, church activities, or others? What do you get out of being a part of these groups?

## Category 5: General Knowledge Funds

1. Have you ever traveled to other places? Where? Why?
2. What did you learn by traveling to other places?
3. What are your favorite places to visit? Why?
4. Where would you travel if you could go anywhere you wanted? Why? What would you do there?
5. What are the most important things happening in the world today? Why are these most important for you?
6. Who are the most important or influential people in the world today? Why do you think they are important?
7. What makes you want to pay attention to current events?
8. What makes you decide to ignore a news story? What makes you want to learn more?
9. What makes you want to learn something new? When you want to learn something, how do you usually do it? What helps you learn? What, if anything, doesn't help when you are learning new things?
10. Whom do you learn the most from? What makes them good teachers for you?

## FUNDS OF KNOWLEDGE AS A KEY, NOT A REPLACEMENT

Using students' funds of knowledge is *not* intended to replace instructional design procedures or traditional assessments, but to enhance them both. We will discuss those procedures at length in Chapter 6. But as Johnston and Costello (2005) find, "Assessment is a social practice that involves *noticing, representing, and responding* to children's literate behaviors, rendering them meaningful for particular purposes and audiences" (p. 258, emphasis added). Many traditional resources still used for teaching youth can become obsolete when used on their own in contemporary classrooms if they are not responsive to students' identities. They can be made useful only if teachers have the data to link those resources and tasks explicitly and meaningfully to students' current knowledge and experiences.

None of this means traditional resources lack value; on the contrary, they can and should be used when they are useful. The key is for professionals to use resources purposefully rather than based on unexamined tradition or assumption. They *might* be useful for teaching a certain group the concepts, skills, and practices they need to participate in contemporary society. But the curricular content they often serve is unlikely to be sufficient, especially if students are not already engaged by the topics. As Moje et al. (2004) find, academic resources used with no connection to daily life can *prevent* learning. Thomas and Oldfather (1997) note when we plan tasks that ignore, discount, or subordinate students' interests, practices, and experiences in favor of requiring them to learn using only the academic resources we choose without their input, we set those students up to fail. Connecting new learning to students' prior knowledge is the key to their developing new understandings, meanings, and uses from academic practice (Monnin, 2009).

## ASSESSING FUNDS OF KNOWLEDGE:
## A CONTINUOUS PROFESSIONAL PRACTICE

If there is any unavoidable "rule" about using funds of knowledge data for instructional design, it is that teachers must recognize that students' funds are constantly changing. As students grow (and they grow fast!), their home lives change. Students may move, and thus their communities may change, or they might live in neighborhoods that are re-developed or shifting economically in ways that change the conditions of their day-to-day lives. What's popular in "pop culture" with students one month (or week, or day) changes faster than most teachers can track, and what students might care about now in relation to the larger world is always dependent on multiple factors, including culture, class, and even simple access to information and opportunity.

In other words, using FoK data cannot and must never be allowed to serve as a "one and done" strategy. Teachers habitually must ask and re-ask students, observe behavior, engage with new media and popular culture their students consume, and consistently revise and refine data sets about what students know and do over time. Doing so ensures teachers can purposefully use data that *actually* engage their current students in ways that are meaningful to them as well as academically sound.

## CONCLUSION

Having offered a rationale for assessing students' funds of knowledge, in Chapter 5 we offer a Model Unit Plan in mathematics to demonstrate how it can be used to design instruction. We then describe in Chapter 6 how to generate purposeful unit-level plans that are responsive to students' identities and needs, and support instructional continuity. Such design is more likely to be successful than traditional academic-based planning and mere logical procedure without consideration of actual learners' strengths and needs. We again emphasize that the design structures we present are not revolutionary. But together they empower teachers to purposely generate what more traditional procedural models do not: a framework that succeeds because it places learners at the center and explicitly responds to them and their needs rather than forcing them to respond to us and our assumed expectations.

But what does it *look like*?" one might ask. That is an excellent, sincere question.

In order to clearly illustrate what teaching on purpose looks like in real practice, following each chapter that describes an element of purposeful teaching, beginning with this chapter, is a Model Unit Plan featuring that element in an instructional design written by a practicing teacher in a major secondary grades content area: math, social studies, science, and English. We ask readers to note that while our guest authors were among the people who vigorously agreed with us that purposeful plans must include certain basic structures and details, you will likely notice that each uses purposeful teaching elements and design structures in different ways. That includes occasionally *not* using some structures *on purpose*. Each Model Unit Plan is slightly different and reflects one professional's work to respond and teach on purpose. We encourage all readers to do the same and use the ideas and framework we offer here flexibly, adaptively, and as needed to succeed and help students learn well. We are all professionals, and there is no single process or template for making a quality instructional plan. The first of those four model teaching units is found in the next chapter and focuses on using funds of knowledge that students bring to a math class.

# CHAPTER 5

# Model Unit Plan 1

## Using Funds of Knowledge to Engage Students in Learning Mathematical Functions

*Maureen Cavalcanti,*
*University of Kentucky*

I never teach my pupils. I only attempt to provide the conditions in which they can learn.

—Albert Einstein

### MODEL UNIT PLAN:
### TEACHING STUDENTS ABOUT FUNCTIONS IN MATHEMATICS

Functions are everywhere. How do we use functions to make sense of real-world problems? There is no short answer. An instructional unit for building understanding about mathematical functions helps students develop their own conceptual understandings of knowledge and skills and standards. And they do that by working with me to model how functions get used in their personal worlds every day. Why does modeling with functions in personal contexts matter? The National Council of Teachers of Mathematics (NCTM, 2009) explains why engaging in mathematical modeling is important:

> Mathematics should help students understand and operate in the physical and social worlds. They should be able to connect mathematics with a real-world situation through the use of mathematical models. The connections between mathematics and real-world problems developed in mathematical modeling add value to, and provide incentive and context for, studying mathematical topics. (p. 2)

The term *function* itself is used in many contexts in and outside of mathematics. Whether they are in the mathematics classroom, a place of employment, or their community, individuals can use functions to make sense of our world through, for instance, the process of modeling.

If this were an episode of *Sesame Street*, and *function* was the word of the day, maybe Leonardo DiCaprio would be the celebrity guest and a *Sesame Street* character like Grover would act out examples of what a function is and what it means to function. Some of those examples might include the idea that when we do a chore at home we perform a function, or when I drink my cup of coffee in the morning I am able to function.

Alternatively, for every city block we walk to school, we burn *y* number calories, so there is a relationship between the total number of blocks we walked and the total number of calories we burned to walk that far (the number of calories burned is a *function* of the number of blocks walked). In class, *Sesame Street* may not be relevant for older students, but it might be the perfect way to help them use a familiar media text, in this case the TV episode, to realize they already know about and live based on functions every day, not just in math class. Depending on the data I collect to find out who my students are and what they do and know beyond school, TV shows like *Family Feud* or *Top Gear* might be better suited for instructional resource use in a secondary mathematics classroom. The key to my designs is *knowing* that my students' lives and experiences themselves are the larger context of my work as a math teacher, and thus the actual focus of my planning for a unit on identifying, building, and interpreting functions.

### Using Contextual Data to Design Instruction

Who are my students? The only answer to that question that stays the same year after year is that they are *my kids*. This is as true of my students from classes 10 years ago as of my students 5 years ago and even my college students from 1 year ago—some of whom are older than me. It is a mindset I've developed and fostered over 10 years. A decade into my career, I am still learning lessons "my kids" from my first year teaching in Los Angeles taught *me* about who they are and how they learn. I left that job after 1 year and I often ask myself, if I were there now, what kind of teacher would I be? Would I feel more successful now than I did then? But I also think about how the notion of funds of knowledge to focus my teaching purposefully was so embedded in my professional thinking from that point forward, and not just because my doctoral program was driven by a focus on educational research about teaching diverse students for social justice. I always looked for social entry points to connect with my students and provide them every opportunity to engage in mathematics. But I was a novice then. I didn't always know how to use knowledge of my students as purposefully as I might have to plan for success through responsive teaching. The model I offer in this chapter helps demonstrate how as an experienced educator I use students' funds to teach them today.

### Introducing the Unit—Going Viral

I have chosen to present a unit on functions for a few reasons. The Common Core State Standards currently used in many U.S. states frame the subject of math so that functions are grouped in their own separate domain, and as a result it is not obvious how to translate the language of the Common Core into instructional practice. There is additionally the connection to mathematical modeling, also its own domain within the Common Core and included in other quality state standards, wherein modeling provides real-world application of functions as mathematical concepts. There are rich opportunities for students to choose how they demonstrate their learning.

I have taught units on functions in three very different settings: high school Algebra 1, test preparation, and a college-level undergraduate course for preservice math teachers. The numerous differences within and across those settings have required me to be purposefully responsive in my design and to constantly revise based on who my students are and what they need in their particular context. Most important, those revisions have helped me realize many rich ways to use funds of knowledge data to design mathematics instruction.

I have given the unit rather boring names in past versions, such as, simply, "Functions" or "Family of Functions." Using data about students' funds of knowledge, I now notice and use the strong presence of social media in students' lives to aptly title this unit "Going Viral with Functions," helping me teach them how quickly a message spreads in the digital world, using math to understand it. Those contextual data alone provide me several sincere questions to ask that give students interesting reasons to learn and practice math. For example, how fast does a message spread on social media (e.g., Instagram)? Snapchat and Instagram as social media have themselves gone viral. As popular media tools, they have great power to initially interest most students today. An online graph depicts the number of Facebook users (www.benphoster.com/facebook-user-growth-chart-2004-2010/). Its depiction of growth over time is ripe with opportunities for interpretation in terms of mathematical functions and their relationships in the context of pop culture, which my students know extremely well already, thereby helping them focus on the mathematics while studying it for interesting purposes.

More textual-based multimedia resources could be used, such as www.psfk.com/2011/05/how-did-instagram-grow-so-fast.html, which discusses how the app Instagram became such a popular social media platform that many of my students use as a primary way to communicate every day. Later in the unit, I use information from the data I collected about Instagram having "100,000 users within a week of launching" and having "4.25 million users who post 10 photographs per second," to build lessons that help my students interpret and apply functions in math class both academically and for real life. A third multimedia resource I now use to introduce functions through real-world facts and figures is the *Did You Know?* video presentation series described at shifthappens.wikispaces.com/. I have shared this resource with every class since it first "went online" as a point of conversation because I learned that my students knew, valued, and used wikis to interact online in other aspects of their lives. In fact, I learn quite a bit about my students' interests every time I use those data to refine my instruction as I continue as a professional. That's how I learned Myspace was on its way out, after showing the original version of the video to a class a year after it was created (I'm hip like that). Similarly, I know from funds of knowledge data that most young people are now moving away from Facebook to use social media like Instagram and Snapchat more. It will be my job to learn how I can use those platforms to help teach functions now and in the future.

Asking questions related to personal activity and popular culture funds of knowledge helps me assess the relevance of planning elements as seemingly minor as the unit title, and also select robust instructional vehicles for students to use when learning. Using World Cup soccer as the context for this unit changed student responses to our class's inquiry, for example, and resulted in a different unit title and task sequence the last time I implemented this instruction. Using data showing that my students knew about and valued soccer in their day-to-day lives helped me respond to them by designing a unit about the World Cup of Functions, wherein each different family of functions represented a "team," and the "winner" was essentially the function team most appropriate to use for modeling a situation. I have even applied data about my students' languages to engage them by titling this unit "WTF?" While heads may turn (and administrators quiver), the title is a math question that provokes curiosity about why I would use such a seemingly controversial expression when I truly mean, "What's the function?" Obviously, I work to use school-appropriate language, but my point stands: Just by choosing a topic that my data about students' funds of knowledge tell me is relevant, I can title a unit plan in ways that make it more likely for students to engage and learn well across variable contexts.

The unit as presented here is driven by sincere probing questions that engage students as well as produce generative topics that allow many ways to answer and inquire. The driving question for the unit is, *How can we use functions to model real-world phenomena?* This unit is aimed at engaging Algebra I students and focuses on learning functions and applying that learning to settings that are relevant and meaningful to my students' lives.

### Activating Students' Prior Knowledge—An Algebra 1 Example

While the concept of functions in mathematics may be new for Algebra I students, knowledge of patterns and sequences and reading graphs can go a long way in supporting their learning. My students almost always know and understand more about functions than they realize when they come to class. There is the classic but futile question of what students *should* know and the more useful data I can use about what students *do* know. I would be lying if I denied I've had moments when I asked students to plot a point in the coordinate plane and my response to their blank stares was, "You should know this already!" But that's a habit I can and do work to break every time I teach. I have to remember I'm an expert in my subject and my students are beginners. To get at what *they* already know about functions, I need to assess prerequisite knowledge and skills, including misconceptions they may hold about math. Some popular culture funds of knowledge questions and more peripheral questions related to functions help me get at their understandings and misunderstandings each time I revise and implement this design. I ask questions that include:

- What have you learned about patterns that was meaningful to you?
- What do you like/dislike about functions, patterns, lines, and mathematics in general?
- How can a number be represented in different ways? (Or, a more student-friendly phrasing—Where do you see numbers every day?)
- What kind of relationships can we have in math?
- How fast does . . . grow?

Prerequisite math knowledge for this unit includes familiarity with expressions, patterns, variables, equivalency (e.g., solving equations), graphing $x$ and $y$ values in the coordinate plane given a table of values or ordered pairs, and proportional relationships. Misconceptions related to functions that commonly arise include misunderstanding of the formal definition and specific academic language, difficulties moving between representations, difficulties conceiving of different formulas representing the same function, and beliefs that functions should be definable by a single algebraic formula.

Figuring out how to use what my students already know from beyond class in different contexts to engage them in learning tasks requires that I have access to data about their family and home life funds of knowledge. I often ask:

- What kinds of things do you do with your family when you are together?
- What are your roles in your family?

- What kinds of chores do you and your family members do at home?
- Where did your family come from? What do these origins mean to you and your family?
- What goals do you have for yourself in life?

A student who identifies his or her goal in life as making it to the age of 21 (not unusual among the at-risk students I work with) is likely not interested in problems like the one implied by the famous Peanuts cartoon where Sally states, "Only in math problems can you buy 60 cantaloupes and no one asks what the heck is wrong with you." An obscure problem and math joke about buying 60 cantaloupes would stump *me* if/when students asked, "How will I use this in real life?" other than trying to explain it to them in the context of grocery shopping for a whole gymnastics team. Now, if I had a student like Lucas, whose family came from the south of Brazil, in class, I could engage him by talking about people selling *abacaxi* (pineapples) and *goiaba* (guava) in the middle of the street in traffic. That actually happens, and he knows about it from personal experience. People need to sell *abacaxi* and *goiaba* for a certain price to make a profit. For the buyers, the price may function to make them want to find a better deal from the next vendor. More likely, the number of *goiaba* shoppers can buy will be a function of how much money they have to spend. See? I wasn't lying earlier. Mathematical reasoning is alive and well all around you (don't panic).

I guess that's true even with the more obscure cantaloupe problem in that Peanuts cartoon I described, but notice how I adapted it and made it relevant to life as Lucas lived it instead of forcing him and his classmates to slog through seemingly pointless drills with no connection to their experiences beyond school. The "old school" traditional word problems like the one about mass cantaloupe purchasing obscure the fact that my students really do *use* the math I am teaching all the time. And why obscure that math when I can *use* it to teach my students in contexts that are relevant to them? Learning where they come from and whether that background is important to them, acquiring knowledge of their family structures and dynamics, and finding out about their goals for the future are all worth the time and help me to develop rich mathematical tasks that cannot be found in any textbook. And as teachers know, seeing how a lesson truly connects to a classmate's real-life experiences brings the learning to life for the rest of the students in the class as well.

## Focusing Learning Targets to Increase Success—Five Big Ideas About Functions

The goal of this unit is for students to develop understandings of the five "big ideas" about functions:

- The function as a mathematical concept
- Covariation and rate of change
- Families of functions
- Combining and transforming functions
- Multiple representations of functions (Lloyd, Beckmann, Zbiek, & Cooney, 2010 )

In Algebra I, and even more so in a single unit, the depth of that understanding will not be fully achieved and is not my purpose. For instance, while linear, quadratic, and exponential functions may be appropriate in this unit to develop essential understandings, I assess for my students that power functions, period functions, and logarithmic functions would be better suited for later exploration into deeper and more sophisticated math practices. That being said, those more complex families of functions could arise in this unit when we look at real-world problems. For example, many problems about population growth make it seem as if we are dealing with exponential growth. However, logistical growth, discussed in precalculus, calculus, or physics courses, is a more appropriate way to model population growth than exponential functions. This is where a discussion of domain and range, for instance, becomes relevant. We can make more sense of population growth using families of functions the students have already learned about by restricting the domain to a few introductory families that students who otherwise might feel overwhelmed can successfully manage, understand, and use to build self-efficacy. If the target is long-term learning in mathematics, I can't steer away from the mathematics that naturally arises as a consequence of discussing the concepts being learned in the classroom in relation to students' lived experiences. Some experiences will be more appropriate than others for building mathematical understanding, and I can use data about my students to make that decision if I approach the topic purposefully with students' identities and needs foremost in my mind.

### Generating Relevant Learning Tasks

With respect to practice, mathematics teachers can make tasks rich as a direct result of using students' personal, community, social, and familial backgrounds. But then there are those tasks that are important but lack obvious relevance to life beyond classroom routine, such as starting class with two or three warm-up questions that connect the previous day's instruction to the new topics students will study next. In such cases, I find value in strategic use of directed practice, such as using input–output tables. Input–output and graphical representations commonly are identified as the most familiar aspects of functions for students, but understanding concepts through, for instance, input–output may limit students to procedural understanding.

Starting this unit by giving students an input–output table and asking them to graph points from the table or find a pattern within the input values and a pattern within the values of the output serve clear and explicit purposes in my classroom. It's a way for me to assess students' skills and knowledge of content without adding written text, which may compromise their ability to answer the question being asked (and their ability to figure out what question is being asked in the first place!). There is an intentional focus on reading and interpreting text as part of the problem-solving process, but that is not the focus of my instruction at that moment in the unit. The directed practice and warm-up are necessary, but it is a quick formative assessment I'm looking for, and I have very specific skills I want to assess for student understanding so I design this task for that purpose.

For instance, when I begin teaching this unit I want to know to what extent students are able to plot values from the input–output tables by associating an input value with an output value and identifying a location in the coordinate plane found by using the input values as a horizontal distance and the output values as a vertical distance from the origin. For those readers who do not teach math, I will pause so you can recover from the stroke I just induced in your brain. I promise what I just wrote was a real sentence about math. The point is that by offering this pre-assessment purposely as a strategic introduction, I can learn a lot about what my students already know about functions, what they need to learn, and how I might design later learning tasks so they will be more successful.

Lessons in this unit are sequenced to engage students in purposeful mathematical tasks that provide opportunities for them to acquire knowledge and practice skills related to the concept of functions, including:

1. Determining whether a relation is a function. A relation is a kind of function if variables $x$ and $y$ are placed in a group of ordered pairs. If object $x$ is from the first set and object $y$ is from the second set, then the objects are said to be related. Defining functions and using language associated with that definition is essential (input–output, ordered pairs, domain and range, $x$- and $y$-values, independent and dependent variables).
2. Writing a formula for a function (e.g., explicitly, recursively).
3. Using various representations to represent and interpret functions.
4. Interpreting functions in real-world contexts.

These lesson-level tasks help me focus and specify the primary learning targets for the unit overall and sequence them in a logical way for my students, which in turn helps me ensure I fully teach and assess them in ways that help them reach those targets, learn, and thereby meet the standards for mathematical understanding.

## LESSONS AT A GLANCE

### Lesson 1 Overview: When can I classify a relation as a function?

*Learning Targets:*

1. Distinguish between relations that are functions and those that are not functions.
2. Explain how functions work using mathematical terminology, including domain and range.

### Lesson 2 Overview: How should I move?

This lesson has been adapted from Math Shell (map.mathshell.org), Representing Functions of Everyday Situations and NCTM Illuminations (illuminations.nctm.org/), How Should I Move?

*Learning Targets:*

1. Graph a function given a verbal description.
2. Describe the features of a graph (increasing/decreasing, rate of change, continuous/discrete variables, intercepts).

*Vehicles and Purpose:* To start, students sketch a graph that describes the following situation:

- Painting the bridge—A group of workers are planning to paint a bridge.
  - » X = the number of workers
  - » Y = the length of time it will take the workers to paint the bridge

Students show their answers on a mini-whiteboard, or where available the Education Interactive Whiteboard app for iPad, where their work can be saved for future reference. Students are instructed to be prepared to explain their drawings and reasoning while solving the problem. Students often come up with a range of answers. When this is the case, I draw a few on the board and discuss which are appropriate models for the situation, and we analyze the problems and proposed answers together and reason out the most appropriate responses.

Next, students use calculator-based rangers (CBRs) or other motion detectors to physically model various graphical representations of functions. Those include linear (similar to the initial class bridge problem), quadratic, and exponential functions. It could be fun to toss in step or piecewise functions. If graphic calculators and motion detectors are not available, a stopwatch and ruler can suffice but will take much more time because graphing needs to be done manually in that case. It takes time to provide instruction for using the calculators and CBRs, but having students physically move around the classroom to understand rate of change and relate that to specific families of functions provides a shared interactive experience to support learning, so the time is worthwhile.

### Lesson 3 Overview: Should we cut down trees?

This lesson is adapted from Goldberg (2007).

*Learning Targets:*

1. Write an explicit formula using recursive methods.
2. Make conjectures and investigate problems using patterns and repeated reasoning.
3. Interpret solutions in the context of the problem.
   a. *Additionally,* distinguish between ways of representing a function, including the connection to sequences and recursively defined functions.

**Vehicle and Purpose:** To start, pose the problem: You are a forest ranger in charge of a national forest that currently has 1,000 trees. A new policy for cutting and planting has just been approved. At the end of each year, 20% of the trees in the forest will be cut down and 100 new, fast-growing trees will be planted. In this lab, you will discover the long-term effects on the number of trees in a forest when people implement a cutting and planting process in which 20% of the trees are cut down at the end of each year and 100 new trees are planted. Figure out the long-term effects of this environmental policy. Will all the trees eventually disappear, will the forest be overgrown with too many trees, or will the result be in between these extremes? These questions give students practice in recognizing other instances where numbers may be presented in manipulative ways in order to promote a particular agenda or course of action, and in evaluating and interpreting the meaning of the numbers presented. Multimedia tools can be incorporated to engage students in investigating this topical problem, including:

- Text-driven Socratic Seminar (potential readings below):
  » Purdue University. (2009, December 9). Logging effects vary based on a forest's history, climate. ScienceDaily. Retrieved from www.sciencedaily.com/releases/2009/12/091202114046. htm
  » USDA Forest Service—Pacific Southwest Research Station. (2014, January 6). *79 years of monitoring demonstrates*

dramatic forest change. ScienceDaily. Retrieved from www.
sciencedaily.com/releases/2014/01/140106133257.htm
»   University of Washington. (2010, December 8).
Bringing the greenback. Conservation. Retrieved from
conservationmagazine.org/2010/12/bringing-the-greenback/
• Television—Use of popular television series such as AxMen and
Swamp Loggers to develop narrative of lumberjack/forestry
practices.

Work to dissect the problem is accomplished using mixed teacher-guided
and student-directed methods. The teacher guides students through a KWL
(What We Know, What We Want to Know, What We Learned) graphic
organizer for the problem. Then students move into groups using a method
appropriate for the given class' work and roles/tasks required to solve the
problem.

***Discussion of Results and Explanation of Mathematical Procedures:*** The
following terminology is discussed in the context of the tree problem (examples will be provided as needed; connections to prior learning will be
consistently made):

• Function
• Recursively defined functions
• Closed form or an equation (including linear functions)
• Input and output (revisit domain and range)
• Conjecture and hypothesis

**Lesson 4 Overview: How do representations help conceptualize the function
concept?**

**Learning Targets:**

1. Match graphs, equations, tables, and rules that represent the same
function and explain your reasoning.

***Vehicles and Purpose:*** Students will explore various representations
of functions in pairs or small groups. At this point in the unit students
have practiced identifying relations that are functions, writing formulae
for recursive relationships (reminiscent of middle school introductions to
sequences), and interpreting graphs of linear, quadratic, and exponential
functions. In this practice set, students are tasked with working collaboratively to match functions represented in four different forms—tabular,
graphical, algebraic, and verbal description. To help connect to previous

lessons involving that practice, there are a number of basic probing questions the teacher must ask:

- Can you group these functions in a way that will help you match them?
- Which of these functions are linear? Nonlinear?
- Which are increasing/decreasing?
- Where does this function cross the x-axis/y-axis? Show me a function that never crosses the x-axis. How do you know?
- Show me a function that intersects the origin. How do you know?
- Show me a function that has two x-intercepts. How do you know?
- Where does this function reach its maximum/minimum value?

After completing the function sorting, students engage in cooperative learning tasks, such as a *gallery walk* in which they move around the room and review other groups' posted findings. Students use Post-its to write questions and comments about group choices of matches, as shown on their posters. Students then return to their original groups and their works to read through student feedback. Whole-class discussion of results and new understandings follow. Any functions students have questions about are discussed in more detail.

**Lesson 5 Overview: How can I predict my future with functions?**

*Learning Targets:*

1. Find a pattern in both the domain and range of a given function, identify the family of function from the pattern (linear, quadratic, exponential), and support choice of functions by plotting points and describing the resulting graph of the function.
2. Determine alternative methods for determining a family of functions from a domain and range when a pattern is not obvious.

***Vehicles and Purpose:*** Ask students probing questions related to growth and decay such as, "What continues to grow or shrink over time quickly?" "Where do you see something getting larger or smaller at a constant rate?" Give examples such as the tree in the forest problem, the spread of Ebola, the effect of vaccination rates, amount of time spent traveling to school over a month, and so on. Ask students what they would do if they were given a table of values and asked to predict a future value. For comic relief, and to introduce the importance of having multiple points to determine the family of a function, the teacher can present the following comic from XKCD or a variation posed as a problem like: Yesterday your dog had no puppies. To-

**Figure 5.1. Extrapolating (Fun)ctions in Mathematics**

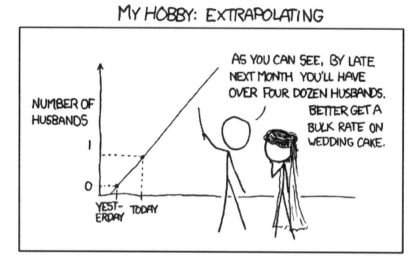

*Source:* www.xkcd.com

day she has five. By late next month at this rate she will have approximately how many puppies? (see Figure 5.1).

Have students share observations of patterns that arose in the domain and range. Here would be a good time to use technology such as Desmos (free) or TI-nspires ($) by having students plot points and describe patterns they see in the graph itself and how those might support conclusions drawn from the patterns they determined by the table of values. Microsoft Excel ($), open office (free), or Google sheets (free) also could be used to identify patterns in the domain and range of a function, given an input–output table.

Additional multiple media resources that could be incorporated into this unit:

- Storytelling: *The King's Chessboard* by D. Birch (1993) can be used as an example of function patterns, namely, exponential growth.
- Videos about functions
    » Silly video: www.youtube.com/watch?v=_hQF_4wHkEA
    » Very silly video: www.youtube.com/watch?v=E2vJ0Jo3iqc
    » Not suitable for all audiences: www.youtube.com/watch?v=VUTXsPFx-qQ
    » Math Dude: www.youtube.com/watch?v=qjVB07yN5VE
    » "Functions in the Real World": www.educationworld.com/a_curr/mathchat/mathchat010.shtml

## CONCLUSION

The funds of knowledge I collected and used to design my teaching in my first year honestly scared me sometimes, especially when they made their way into my classroom in the form of violence or when students' behavior frustrated me and led me to believe they didn't care. With experience, I now understand what a poor characterization of their behavior my youthful perceptions were. Apathy is unfortunately still alive and well in math class, but it can't be any purposeful teacher's default interpretation that student responses indicate they are lazy or don't care. My job is to find out how to use what students know and what they are doing, to identify opportunities for teaching them math. And yes, there is math in everything. Don't listen to all that nonsense about how nobody uses algebra in real life. Mathematics is literally like the premise of the now-classic movie *The Matrix*. We live in a world that can be explained and even created using numbers and calculations and coded patterns. My job is to position students to swallow the red pill, stay in "wonderland" with me, and come on an adventure down the rabbit hole we call "Math." (Spoiler alert: It's a really deep and interesting rabbit hole!)

# CHAPTER 6

# Planning Purposeful Instruction for Successful Teaching and Learning

The best laid schemes of mice and men
Go often askew . . . .

—Robert Burns, "To a Mouse"

## INTRODUCTION

To paraphrase Robert Burns's famous poem, no matter our good intentions, the best laid plans of mice and men often go wrong. Promises of happy endings sometimes lead us down roads that are, to mix metaphors, paved with those . . . um . . . good intentions and lead us to places we never want to visit. Any honest teacher with experience can tell countless stories about times she bled, cried, and perspired to plan activities, assignments, and lessons to create near-three-ring-circus-grade units that surely would succeed. Then she put those plans in action and watched horrified as students swarmed the plans and made chaos of them.

Teachers are mere mortals. We mean well, and we usually plan at least a little for what will happen in our classes. But planning isn't the same as teaching. Some people who've successfully taught "by the seat of their pants" will loudly say planning doesn't matter if you just know your stuff. And sometimes that works for highly experienced teachers. But not always for them and rarely for the rest of us. Purposeful teaching is the opposite of teaching by the seat of your pants. It's the thinking and strategy that make good teaching possible. Planning is what makes successful teaching not just possible but likely.

Planning can be tedious. It is always complex. It's hard to plan well—logically and manageably—to teach a topic, skill, concept, or practice to a group of children who may not all be focused on or interested in what you offer. Because planning can eat time, a lot of teachers abandon its fullest use in favor of outlines, mini-lessons, and activities that fill time and lend themselves well to prepackaged textbook work that (supposedly) already has done the purposeful, responsive design work a professional educator requires.

Many teachers learn to plan detailed instruction during their preservice preparation programs only to abandon the high levels of structure required when confronted with the apparent need to teach in "triage" mode, wherein occasional classroom conditions or temporary school environments disrupt prepared plans and require some degree of improvisation and even temporary abandonment of prepared plans. But some teachers teach in this mode as a matter of preference. And although triage teaching often *looks* similar to highly planned classroom instruction, triage teachers can rarely make decisions as purposefully as the teachers who truly plan. The triage teacher's decisions might be *momentarily* purposeful and apparently effective, but in the long term the teacher who plans on purpose is more likely to succeed, not least because when moments of triage arise in that teacher's classroom (and they will). That teacher has a *plan* that will guide and help the class remain on course. Triage teachers can only patch up situations and hope whatever's bleeding isn't so serious that the lesson will die.

A purposeful, professional, responsive plan is a teacher's most powerful tool—not only for teaching and assessing content, but for creating classroom environments that correlate with engaged learning, fewer and less serious classroom management incidents, higher levels of student learning, and more successful curriculum and instruction overall. Without a plan, you are headed upstream without a paddle. To paraphrase famed author Victor Hugo, people who plan provide a thread that helps them navigate the maze of life. We strongly recommend the following detailed approach so teachers can make decisions with good reason and productive ends constantly in mind.

## PURPOSEFUL PLANS: BASIC DESIGN ELEMENTS

### Unit-Level Planning and Structures

We recommend teachers design instruction with the long term in mind, especially when focused on creating individual lessons for a day or a week to cover just one or two concepts, skills, or practices in a content area. Like others, including Wiggins and McTighe (2005), we advocate using clear, *sincere* questions as anchor points, themes, or vehicles for inquiry and discussion (see Chapter 8). We also advocate using questions as vehicles to connect as much academic work as possible to real-life tasks and purposes that the teacher has systematically documented as valuable and meaningful for the particular students she seeks to teach (see Chapter 4).

We recommend teachers in all subject areas consistently offer students explicit learning goals that do more than state the learning targets for the unit and lessons but also explain *why* those goals and targets matter, *what* students will use to meet those targets, and *how* that learning will be useful in life. We further recommend teachers purposefully identify and select a wide array of textual resources using multiple media to provide students with a large and interesting variety of texts to choose from and use while engaged in learning (see Chapters 3 and 10).

At the lesson level, we recommend focusing each lesson on two or three specific objectives. This has two purposes. First, focusing learners on practice and mastery of two or three related and manageable elements of a subject area makes learning easier for students without dumbing down the content. For example, in science classrooms, students often study the structure of a living cell. This frequently includes learning about structures like membranes, mitochondria, endoplasmic reticulum, ribosomes, the nucleus, and related topics like osmosis, mitosis, meiosis, and other processes. Traditional biology classes typically teach all of these things at once and test students for their ability to quickly memorize the names, shapes, and functions of each cell; explain why each matters; understand how osmosis works; and figure out how cells reproduce and grow to form living organisms. That's a lot to learn all at once! It can be so much that many learners reach a point of frustration—the point at which their brains very literally cannot hold all the required information. And even if they do, the next lesson brings a similarly heavy conceptual and vocabulary load and can overwhelm them.

When learners' brains reach the level of cognitive frustration, learners often disengage and give up. They simply can't handle it. As purposeful teachers, we might productively break down this collection of structures, terminology, functions, and phenomena into more manageable chunks and plan in ways that present it all so our students can learn, understand, use, and master key elements in smaller bites; build their efficacy; and then move on in the curriculum to learn more with confidence.

Second, chunking instruction and scaffolding plans in logical but focused sequences of manageable cognitive target sets and formative learning tasks enables us to focus on assessing *only the targets we specified* for learning in a particular lesson.

A *cognitive learning target* is an explicitly stated and clearly explained academic goal specifying the cognitive acts required for engagement (identification, analysis, application, etc.); a clear description of the content-area skills, concepts, and/or practices to be learned; how those will be practiced; and ideally a brief reference to the purpose of attaining the target. It encompasses more than the looser term *target*, which has become common in place of other traditional terms like *objectives*, *outcomes*, *goals*, and other ways of describing the desired results of instruction. A cognitive learning target is more than an "I can" statement or an assertion of what students will be able to *do* as the result of instruction. For example, "I can use primary sources to explain historical events," is an "I can" statement about a narrow outcome of student learning in social studies. However, even a purposeful learning target lacks several elements of a purposeful *cognitive* learning target, which would constitute an explicit learning goal, as described in Chapter 6. We recommend using what we refer to as statements of cognitive learning targets like the example below to ensure purposeful planning.

A cognitive learning target states more than the *activity* and/or topic(s) students will be expected to learn. It states the particular *cognitive* skills the students must use (identify, comprehend, apply, analyze, synthesize, evaluate, and more), the concept(s) and/or skill(s) to be learned, the resources that will be used, and the purpose. As such, a purposeful revision of the "I can" objective offered above generates a target like this:

> Students will practice and learn to identify, analyze, and explain uses of primary source texts to interpret historical facts and events. Using *The Federalist Papers* and the collected letters of James Madison, and the textbook for this class, students will evaluate how historians use primary sources to develop knowledge in order to understand that historical thinking is a process of evidence-based interpretation.

Yes, cognitive learning targets are more complex. That is on purpose, and that purpose is the element that ensures professionals design plans that are precise, explicitly relevant, and responsive to themselves, to the subjects they teach, and especially to the students they educate.

Similarly, we purposely use the technical phrase *formative learning task* instead of "activity" to discuss procedures or experiences used to teach academic content, especially in the context of lesson plan procedures. It has become a kind of shorthand for teachers to talk about what they do in terms of "doing activities" (e.g., "I did this great activity with my students where we learned how to use primary sources in history class. It's really fun and they love it!"). Sometimes, activity can be purposeful learning. However, thinking this way as a professional leads to a constant pitfall in the logic of teaching. Activity simply means doing something. And while everything we ask our students to do in classrooms constitutes "activity," that activity is not always necessarily connected in sufficiently intentional ways to enhance learning. For that to be true, professionals must formulate formative learning tasks. These formative tasks are, as noted, highly explicit regarding what teachers and students will do in terms of learning, practicing, and using cognitive skills. They specify concepts and practices students will learn to participate in and perform in class, and they explain the reasons why each task is relevant to student success.

None of this is to argue we should all toss out every fun *activity* we've ever used. Not at all. It means that, if we are purposeful, we always frame those activities as interesting *tasks* that are explicitly designed to help students succeed in a step-by-step process toward mastering a fundamental element of their education. If the formative learning tasks are based on students' funds of knowledge and connect academic content to real life in meaningful ways, they will still result in "fun" a lot of the time. Fun is really a function of *interest* in learning processes, and interest is a function of responsive teaching. Therefore, using cognitive targets and formative learning tasks is much more than inventing new jargon for teachers to trip over. *Targets* and *tasks* are more precise professional terms for the work we actually do.

Focusing and sequencing targets and tasks has a practical benefit for both teachers and students. By chunking and sequencing targets, tasks, and assessments according to strategically limited sets of clear and logical goals across a unit of instruction, we can focus our assessments, feedback, and grading on just a few aspects of the curriculum at a time. Rather than grading 120 (or 200 or more) student reports on *everything* about cell structure at once, a biology teacher instead can assess two or three key elements of that topic at a time. That allows the teacher to provide students with feedback that doesn't overwhelm them and helps them understand more, and enables the class to move more systematically through the curriculum. When we logically sequence lessons in a unit with these chunks, students more ably focus on a few things at a time, understand more quickly, perform more successfully sooner, and feel greater self-efficacy when asked to learn more. In turn, the teacher's planning positions her to be efficient in assessing student learning while still providing rich feedback. The difference is a matter of strategy. A matter of purpose.

With all this in mind, a unit plan is a purposely designed series of lessons focused on a particular topic required for academic success in classroom learning, as well as preparation for use of that knowledge in life beyond school. We can usefully think of a unit plan as a giant lesson plan. Each lesson plan (1) is one step in that giant plan designed to provide students with logical sets of cognitive learning targets, (2) implements those targets to guide teaching and learning, and (3) uses relevant formative tasks sequenced in manageable steps to ensure students succeed at optimal levels every step of the way toward summative assessment(s) and mastery. Each step in the design is a task or set of tasks that helps students learn concepts, practice skills, and apply new knowledge they need to master in order to grow, move forward, meet standards, and succeed on summative assessments by the end of the unit at higher levels than they would have if the unit were not planned so carefully.

This approach means that teaching a school subject is never a matter of tricking students into learning, or "catching" students who might not be engaged, or otherwise requiring students to guess what's required for their success or respond to unspoken expectations about what they are supposed to do. It is the opposite of triage teaching. Purpose and passion go extremely well together, though, and in fact purpose enables passion to shine in a teacher's classroom performance. That said, when we teach with passion but without a purposeful plan, we only hope for the best. When we design instruction as recommended in this chapter, and when we make the purposes explicit to our students, we all succeed more.

## Planning for Successful Instruction: Parts and Purposes

In the following section we briefly discuss the basic structures of a typical unit plan, with one addition: We discuss the purposes of these parts and advocate that teachers rely on *purpose* more than procedure as they work. A unit plan (or a lesson) can be designed in many different ways and still be used to successfully teach. There is no single, can't miss "Step 1" every teacher must begin with when planning. There is no universal format perfect or necessary for everyone to use in the same ways at the same time, and we strongly caution readers to resist temptations to standardize what we offer here into any prescription for designing units and lessons they believe must be "right." There are many "right" ways to teach well. As the Model Unit Plans in this book illustrate, purposeful and engaging units take many shapes.

We also emphasize that the sequencing of a unit's or lesson's structures might usefully vary across content areas, and recognize professionals can and should change the order of the parts depending on their goals for being responsive in their classrooms. Planning can be standardized, and we've seen what that looks like and how it affects students and teachers (negatively). When planning follows standardized procedures or requires professionals to include certain structures in certain orders in certain ways every time, the results are harmful due to simple facts. No two people *ever* learn, understand, perceive, experience, and act in the same ways at the same times for the same reasons at the same rate to the same depth all the time, every time. Ever. Basic human variation ensures that treating students as if learning *does* work that way will result in certain students succeeding more than others, and that result will be based almost entirely on chance. With a plan designed for student success on *purpose*, more learners are more likely to learn better, deeper, faster, and sooner than when their teachers simply hope their passion will be inspiration enough.

Standardized planning may often be worse than lack of planning at all, because by definition standardized planning and their implementation prevent responsive teaching, plain and simple. Professionals cannot be responsive to diverse students if the instructional designs they must use don't account for diversity and variation. More than that, it gives the people they serve a false impression there is some perfect recipe that will result in successful education if we will all just toe the line and follow the "right" way. That notion runs counter to nearly everything educators know about how people learn and how good teaching works.

That said, we acknowledge that the parts of units and lessons are just that—the parts. They matter, they're fundamental, and they have remained stable enough over time that the basic building blocks of unit and lesson plans can be usefully represented, as shown in Figure 6.1).

## Unit Title

To begin designing a purposeful unit, we recommend teachers first identify what has been referred to as a generative topic (Blythe & Associates, 1998)—a topic that enables multiple perspectives, discussion of related and new/emerging topics, divergent questions, with no single or universal set of "right" answers overall. It should be authentically meaningful and/or valuable to students who will use the unit to learn. After identifying the generative topic(s) for study, we recommend composing an actual title for each unit that cues students, informs them of the unit's purpose, and focuses attention on new concepts, skills, and practices they will learn. No unit should ever be titled simply according to its topic (for example, "Reproduction" or "Population Growth"). Rather, unit titles should be students' first encounter with their explicit learning goal(s). For example, instead of "Reproduction," we might title a unit in science using a generative title like this: "Be Fruitful and Multiply: How Different Organisms Make New Life." Similarly, rather than titling a social studies unit "Population Growth," we might generatively title it "The Weight of the World: How the Number of People in the World Affects Our Planet." Yes, we recognize this is more involved. It also makes the title a purposeful instructive element of the plan. It literally tells the students (and us as teachers) what we're studying and provides the first thread to guide classroom work.

## Unit-Level Concepts, Skills, and Practices to Be Learned and Assessed

After establishing a generative title, teachers can review students' knowledge of the unit topic(s), along with available or desired instructional resources, to identify the concepts, skills, and practices students must be taught, allowed to practice, and demonstrate mastery of to prove understanding. It is important to distinguish between "skills" to be taught, and concepts to be taught. For example, *identifying* themes is a skill students in English require in order to engage in literary analysis and while reading in everyday life; *analyzing, applying, explaining, writing, demonstrating,* and *comparing* are other skills all teachers target for instruction regardless of subject area. It is important to distinguish between these skills and the "concepts" students will use to practice applying those skills. In this example, students first must understand the concept of theme before they can identify or analyze it. Theme is the concept to be learned, and analysis is the skill to be used for learning it. Without keeping the distinction clear, teachers may fail to make conceptual knowledge explicit, and find themselves teaching without clarity

**Figure 6.1 . Elements of a Purposeful Instructional Plan**

Topic(s):

- What subject-area concepts, skills, and practices will the students practice and learn during this unit? (targets and standards)

Context(s):

- Who are my students?
- What do my students already know about the topic/concept/skill/practices we will study? (funds of knowledge data)
- How can I use what they already know?
- Recommended topics
- Relevant and contemporary resources
- Engaging tasks

Unit Title:

- (Should be an actual title that provides meaningful cues about the purpose of study for students; avoid titles like "Cells," "The Revolutionary War," "To Kill a Mockingbird," or "Polynomials")

Sincere Questions/Issues:

Learning Targets:

- (Concepts, skills, and practices to be learned/assessed):

Formative Learning Tasks and Sequencing:

Textual Vehicles:

- (Specify/identify multiple media; focus on relevance, variety, and choice within structure)

Assessment(s):

- Formative (in process), with clear target alignment and explicit formative learning tasks by lesson
- Summative (benchmark or end-of-unit), with clear relation to formative learning tasks and assessments to optimize student preparation and test reliability [Summative assessments should assess only what has been specifically targeted and taught for student understanding. If it was not explicitly taught, we cannot validly or reliably assess it for student understanding.]

*(continued on next page)*

**Figure 6.1. Continued**

---

Alignment with Standards:

- Any given unit or lesson that is designed on purpose as described in this chapter will (or should) meet any standards-based outcome in any reasonable standards framework for any given content area. As a result, we deliberately do not specify any particular set of content area or national standards for any content area or specific project for local, state, or national education standards.

Lesson Plans:

- A lesson may be designed to take a single class period, or to take multiple days depending on students' needs, subject-matter complexity, school calendar requirements, etc.
- Cognitive learning targets that result in explicit learning goals

Lesson Procedures:

- Routine tasks (What will students routinely do in class each day to ensure their opportunities to participate fully, fairly, and successfully? What routines will be used to complete classroom tasks such as beginning class, discussing in large groups, working in small groups, reviewing, turning in homework, and other logistical issues?)
- Sequence of explicit formative learning tasks

Differentiations, Accommodations, and Modifications:

- What do different students in this group require in order to be successful?
- How do I need to vary learning strategies, teaching methods, and instructional resources to differentiate and meet students' needs?
- What do I need to have or do in order to give additional support to students who may have special needs?
- Is there anything about the lesson content or tasks I need to modify in order to help certain students engage more fully?

---

and coherence to the point where lessons become academically invalid *activity* even when they look like purposeful instruction.

Just as concepts and skills are not the same, neither are skills and practices. For example, solving nonlinear equations in math class requires multiple *skills*, and it also requires that students learn several *concepts* in order to make sense of the processes they must engage in order to solve a problem and *practice* mathematical thinking. In physics class students must learn *concepts* like gravity, speed, motion, and more in order to apply *skills* specified in experimental processes and scientific methods in order to *practice* like scientists to form hypotheses, test them, calculate, interpret, and explain results that help them answer a question or solve a problem. If we as teachers do not make these elements explicit, we cannot teach as purposefully as we would otherwise and we are far less likely to succeed both overall and in particular with the diverse students we work with each day.

## Contexts for Instruction

Next, and essentially, teachers must analyze, identify, and specify the contextual data about their classrooms and students that will influence their logic and decisions for instructional planning that will succeed. As noted in Chapter 4, this is where funds of knowledge data are perhaps most relevant. Whom are we actually teaching? They are more than the sum of their demographic markers; they are individual human beings with real interests, knowledge, values, and concerns. If we want to engage them, we must know as much about how they identify as possible and use those data to inform our questions, targets, tasks, resources, methods, and assessments.

By asking who our students are as the first step in establishing context, we also identify what they already know about the topic to be studied, what prior experiences they have had with it, how they feel about it (do they find it relevant?), and how we can use those data to sequence tasks most logically and refine or refocus topics to optimize engagement. Based on this context, we can begin to identify relevant resources across multiple media and ensure strategic use of both traditional academic *and* contemporary resources to drive instruction. We also can make more informed decisions about which tasks are most likely to work with a certain group of learners (or even an individual) and make additional plans as a result.

## Sincere Questions/Issues

As noted in Chapter 8, we advocate using sincere questions. These are questions that we can ask about the unit topic that will best engage diverse learners in multiple ways that help them explore, learn, and practice with new knowledge in ways that are useful for life beyond school. These questions further help us select resources and identify tasks and sequences with which we know our students are more likely to engage. They position teachers so that we are able to respond depending on how and whether students respond in turn to us. For example, students in a social studies classroom today sometimes struggle to comprehend the ways in which events from centuries ago remain relevant, meaningful, and useful to learn for understanding what is happening in the world today. Using questions to assess students' engagement, teachers become equipped to respond by offering additional instruction about historical events, connecting them to modern representations of the same essential issues and conditions, and thereby utilizing resources and designing tasks that students are more likely to be successful with in learning the social studies skills, concepts, and practices targeted for learning in a lesson or unit.

## Learning Targets, Formative Learning Tasks, and Sequencing

As described earlier, lesson-level cognitive learning targets empower teachers to specify the concepts, skills, and practices they will explicitly teach and assess during a unit. Specifying strategically grouped target sets helps teachers productively limit the scope of each unit and lesson so it is (1) manageable and meaningful for students, and (2) clearly focused on a coherent set of subject-area knowledge. This helps make sure we in fact teach that content and assess it without overwhelming our students (and ourselves) with nonessential, distracting, or confusing elements that otherwise would get in the way or disrupt classroom work.

Regarding sequencing of formative learning tasks, it is possible to consider at least three approaches. We suggest readers use whichever approach is most useful for them and meets their purposes.

First, sequencing of formative learning tasks can be considered in terms of the step-by-step procedures in each lesson. At this level, sequencing means putting formative learning tasks in an order that intentionally and manageably supports students as they are introduced to new content, explore models, discuss them, practice, and complete tasks designed so that students who complete them will be fully prepared for success on the unit's summative assessment. Chapter 7 provides a fully worked out example of what this looks like. This sequencing creates a scaffold—a framework—that the teacher explains to students so they can orient themselves during class to the learning objectives and the steps that will lead to success.

Second, sequencing can be considered in terms of framing each lesson as a formative learning task in itself. At this level, purposeful teachers consider which order of tasks is most logical for students' day-to-day or week-to-week success. The principle of sequencing lessons in this way follows the same logic as sequencing in lesson tasks, which constitute its essential procedural steps, described above. In this case, the teacher simply is using sequences of *lessons* instead of *tasks* to guide students and focus their attention during, between, and across instruction over time until they are prepared to demonstrate mastery of the unit's targets in full.

Third, and importantly, purposeful teachers can consider how separate unit plans can be strategically sequenced to create a throughline or set of themes across an academic year that help students understand how all of the content they study in a course fits together to create a body of knowledge they can *use*—not just in school but in the world—as a way to think, communicate, act, and achieve goals. This large-scale, long-term approach to sequencing also helps teachers design instruction so their work is manageable over extended periods of time, not just in single lessons or a few weeks of instruction at once.

## Textual Vehicles and Instructional Resources

Once the teacher has determined a coherent, manageable, logical sequence of targets and tasks, the next step involves using funds of knowledge data once again to identify, select, and sequence the textual vehicles and resources they determine will be most successful in helping students fully use new knowledge. Noting that variety and choice within structure are essential to engaged learning (see Chapter 3), we recommend teachers use multiple media formats and texts. This includes traditional academic materials such as textbooks, novels, nonfiction, workbooks, and other tools. However, teachers should intentionally apply data about their students' identities to select contemporary texts/topics to be used as central elements of study, too, not just as supplements to textbooks. For details, see Chapter 4.

The key to determining which resources to use in an instructional design is to recognize that we are *not* teaching the resources themselves. A science teacher does not teach some particular textbook but rather the concepts found there, and an English teacher does not (or should not) "teach" a specific author or novel without a purpose in mind. For example, an English teacher might use Shakespeare's *Romeo and Juliet* to teach her students how dramatic texts work, how they are structured, what elements and techniques authors use when they write plays, and how plays work to entertain, inform, and influence audiences, and in the case of Shakespeare, to acquaint them with one of the greatest writers in the language and a story that stays fresh across centuries.

One way to purposefully ensure we do not fall into the trap of teaching texts instead of teaching students is to consistently analyze the tasks and resources we plan to use and ask whether and how they will help students learn specific concepts, skills, and practices *targeted* for assessment, based on students' funds of knowledge data. If the task or resource does not entail focused, relevant attention to a targeted concept, skill, or practice that relates to responsive implementation of that unit, the teacher must consider whether that task/resource should be used. If so, it will require making its purposes in relation to targets, tasks, and assessments explicit and coherent with the rest of the plan. If not, it should be replaced with one that advances student learning toward attainment of the targets we have set for them.

## Assessments

Teachers can productively think about assessment in terms of *formative* and *summative* modes, although we argue that all assessment results should be used in an ongoing formative process to fully teach on purpose. Formative (in-process) assessments focus on determining whether, how, and to what extent students have learned, understood, and succeeded in applying new knowledge related to particular targets stated as focal points in a unit plan. At the lesson level, a teacher might usefully think of each step in a procedure as a moment for formative assessment: Having completed a formative task, did the students understand enough to move on, practice new things, and delve more deeply toward achieving additional learning targets? These formative assessments may be graded, but we do not necessarily advocate that all assessments be evaluative (scored, etc.). Many formative assessments can be derived from observation or discussion with students (formal or informal), and the teacher can then use assessment data to communicate results and make decisions about how to improve, whether to reteach or move on, how to engage at higher levels, or whether it may be necessary to revise elements of the original plan for increased future success.

Summative assessments (end-of-lesson, end-of-unit, or end-of-course) generally consist of larger-scale integrated tests, examinations, and student performances that are evaluative. That is, they are tasks that require students to demonstrate their mastery and level of learning in relation to a given learning target, and they usually are attached to a score or grade used to evaluate individual students' overall success in meeting a classroom or subject area academic standard. Summative assessments are most purposeful and successful when they include *only* tasks that require students to demonstrate the ability to explain knowledge and apply skills or solve relevant problems that were explicitly targeted and taught during the unit/lesson. If a summative assessment includes questions or tasks requiring students to use concepts, skills, or practices that were *not* explicitly taught and practiced, then the summative assessment is neither valid nor reliable. When that happens in a teacher's assessments, the resulting data do not measure whether students succeeded in learning what they were taught. A good assessment must assess what was taught and not test for knowledge, skills, and tasks that were not explicitly taught and never actually practiced. Purposeful instructional design should always ensure the former and prevent the latter.

## Alignment with Standards

All teachers in all subjects are required to document that their teaching aligns with and focuses on attaining certain academic outcomes, often referred to as *standards*. Standards frequently are offered and mandated for teachers to use by subject area professional organizations, the federal government, state governments, local school boards and administrations, and sometimes even particular school buildings, academic departments, or grade-level leaders. We have intentionally avoided discussion of any particular standards framework or education reform movement because when instruction is planned as purposefully as we recommend, it will align with, meet, and likely exceed any reasonable set of academic standards in any content area, whether now or in the future.

Further, we seek to position readers to teach on purpose regardless of what standards are in place at a particular moment in history. Purposeful professionalism is always adaptive and will enable educators to identify how their instructional targets, tasks, assessments, and plans align with standards in any context. As a result, we do not specify subject area or national standards for any field except to note that plans should always include systematic attention to the legal requirements for high-quality education wherever and whenever a teacher may be working, which fundamentally requires us all to ensure our work accounts for standards-based outcomes in our classrooms.

## Lesson Plans

As mentioned earlier in this chapter, lesson plans can be productively thought of as miniature unit plans. The processes teachers use to build lessons are the same as those used for designing units; they simply are focused on smaller micro-elements of a topic, whereas unit plans focus on larger macro-elements over longer periods of time. A lesson may be designed to take a single class period, a couple of days, or multiple days, depending on students' needs, subject-matter complexity, school calendar requirements, and so on. A single lesson should focus on no more than one to three particular learning targets that will prepare students for successful practice, learning, and demonstration of mastery on the unit's summative assessment, and all formative tasks used to complete the lesson should be selected and sequenced explicitly in order to help students acquire the content targeted for learning. In addition, the most purposeful lesson plans include references to routine classroom practices (how to begin class, how to transition from one task to the next, how students are expected to behave, what students should use, how they will demonstrate understanding, and how they will be assessed). These routines help students focus cognitively and learn more *because* they are routine; they are regular, predictable structures, guidelines, and "road signs" students and teachers can use to communicate about what they are doing. Thus they can work more efficiently together toward a clear goal: learning the targeted knowledge for the lesson.

A teacher may sequence formative learning tasks in a lesson very purposefully, but it is important to remember that a plan is just that—a plan. We refer you to our introduction to this chapter to remind you that no plan is perfect. While having a good plan is essential, experienced educators will tell you even the best plans sometimes fail. In fact, *any* quality lesson plan probably will need to be changed repeatedly during instruction in any given classroom because of variables the teacher could not have predicted (for example, unannounced schoolwide fire drills, student misbehavior, other interruptions, or unintended gaps in logic, malfunctioning or inadequate technology, etc.). When necessary, purposeful teachers manipulate task sequences, targets, and assessments in order to respond to students' needs.

Sometimes, for example, it becomes clear a lesson or unit plan isn't working during a class. Perhaps the resources are not adequately engaging for the learners at hand, or the teacher attempted to do too much too quickly, or the students were not prepared to learn the targeted content. If any of these happens, a responsive teacher willingly and actively adapts both in the moment and over time to refine instruction, redresses those problems, and then reteaches. He might alter the task sequence for a day, or switch the order of lessons so learning targets are more logical and manageable. A plan is not a prescription that guarantees success. It is a tool that supports professionals' attempts to attain that success. When we treat plans as prescriptions, we assume one size fits all. In our experience, assuming a plan will work for everyone all the time, no matter what, almost always ends in failure.

### Differentiations, Accommodations, and Modifications

All students are different. Many teachers, including experienced teachers, have questions about what it means to *differentiate* instruction, how to *modify* it, and/or how to *accommodate* learners. What does all this mean? It means being responsive, including at the level of individual student instruction.

*Differentiated* instruction refers to the notion of varying the tasks, resources, sequencing, targets, and/or assessments used with a particular group of students in order to maximize success and respond to students who may have unique, variable, or special needs. For example, no two classes of students are the same even when they are studying the same subject with the same teacher using the same plan. If the teacher is not willing to adapt in response to students, or if the teacher otherwise is unable to do so, many students will not perform at their best. Differentiating instruction can mean, then, adjusting a plan's targets, tasks, resources, and/or assessments in small ways to help students across classes meet the same learning targets in different ways depending on their particular needs. Generally, differentiating instruction does not involve changing the nature of tasks, the complexity of content, or expectations for levels of student attainment of learning targets in terms of quality of performance during assessment.

Similarly, *modification* is a responsive teaching technique intended to make sure teachers adjust their plans and ensure individuals with special needs have the support, structure, and resources they need to participate like their peers. For example, a student with visual problems might require modifications regarding how she uses resources to read during class (using large-print books, enlarged font sizes for worksheets and handouts, having a paraprofessional or collaborating teacher read for/with her, etc.). These changes to planned elements of instruction for a unit or lesson are not intended to alter the targeted content. They are intended to be initiated by the teacher so any students in need are provided reasonable changes that help them learn the same material to the same level of quality as their peers.

Finally, *accommodation is* a term applied when students with formally diagnosed special needs (cognitive, behavioral, physical, social) require different tasks, resources, sequences, methods, assessment formats, or other plans in order to participate, learn, and succeed. Accommodations are different from modifications and differentiations because the latter two do not alter the nature or level of complexity, targets, and tasks a student engages. Accommodations may alter an individual student's targets, the sequence in which they are taught, the tasks the student is required to complete, and how the student will be assessed. Many students with special needs come to class with formal, legal education plans that specify required accommodations and modifications. Accommodations often require teachers to specify the ways they will respond to students when those students' special needs require changes in content and format to optimize quality of learning and classroom experiences.

## CONCLUSION

Purposeful planning is very hard work. We fully recognize that the formats and procedures we describe here demand that professional educators produce highly detailed designs. Such planning is complex and time consuming. However, it is not just the opposite of the "triage" teaching we discussed at the start of this book. Purposeful planning is the *cure*.

While writing about purposeful design, we asked many practicing teachers in leadership positions whether we were asking too much. Were the elements included here all necessary, or were we trying too hard to cover all the bases? Wasn't this all just common sense? If it was too much, how should we respond to the needs of the people we hope read this book?

Our colleagues in public school classrooms all said the same things. *Yes*, this is harder than the kind of "planning" too many teachers often do. We sympathize that it can feel easier to "teach by the seat of your pants" using a few notes about what you are trying to accomplish. It can be exciting to teach that way, and many teachers with a talent for extemporaneous performance find gratification in that approach because it can feel great—when it works. And it can work—sometimes. A fluent, passionate teacher with a few basic ideas, a PowerPoint presentation, and some worksheets occasionally can find success and experience truly happy accidents in which students learn plenty. We love a good impromptu "teachable moment," where the class goes on a tangent to explore an unexpected but important idea or incident, as much as the next teacher (if not more so!).

However, not only did all our colleagues also agree that we need to include everything in this chapter, but they told us it was important to *explain* it as well. If we don't plan like this, they said, we'll never get ahead in our classes. We'll always be doing triage because we'll never be thinking about the bigger picture. And if we stop thinking about that bigger picture, we will forget how. When that happens, we won't be able to call ourselves professionals anymore. If we don't plan like this, we can never teach on purpose. We can only teach by accident, and we are the people responsible for preparing our society's children for life. That's too important to leave to chance. We have to plan like this. We have to teach on purpose.

So we included it all—not just *what* good teachers do when we plan instruction, but *why*. We also, most important, put the learner at the center. Using learners' funds of knowledge requires additional effort and thinking to make successful plans. But it also ensures the success of the students and communities we serve. It requires us to be responsive to the children we work with, and it holds us accountable as professionals. With our students' identities at the center, we can plan in ways no prescription or recipe can accomplish. By fully understanding the parts of our instructional designs, we can work beyond recipes to teach intentionally planned units and lessons we know we can and will adapt, change, refine, adjust, and use more and more fluently over time to make sure every student we meet benefits. In Chapter 7, we demonstrate the power of purposeful sequencing using a Model Unit Plan from science.

# Model Unit Plan 2

## Climate Change and Scientific Literacy

*Barry W. Golden,*
*University of Tennessee, Knoxville*

Although few American classrooms emphasize climate change in their curriculum, this unit, with its broader emphasis on scientific literacy, the need to understand cause/effect, graphic displays of data, and how to communicate an understanding of those data, can be adapted to any class or standard set. To engage in this unit design requires no prior knowledge of climate science (see climate.nasa.gov for resources to quickly learn basic facts), only that students must be prepared to engage with data, logical reasoning, and argumentation in a purposefully sequenced design.

### CLIMATE CHANGE AND CLASSROOM INQUIRY IN SCIENCE

Climate change is a scientific topic and a politically charged social issue that has led to groups taking strong stances about its status as fact, often without attention to or respect for scientific data and the conclusions they inform. This unit gets students to engage in their own scientific inquiries and data analyses so they can draw their own conclusions. To provide my students basic facts to begin learning more, I start the unit by offering these points:

1. The Earth had its highest ever recorded temperatures in 2015, and is likely to break that record in 2016.
2. A number of scientists have stated that global warming might be "paused."
3. Scientists working for Exxon (an oil corporation) concluded fossil fuels have added so much carbon dioxide to the atmosphere that it definitely would lead to warming beyond any natural situation.
4. There is consensus among most climate scientists that the Earth is warming, and humans are the primary cause.

5. A group of climate researchers wrote a letter to the President suggesting Exxon and other fossil fuel companies be investigated for organized crime because of damage their business may have done to the Earth's climate, damage that threatens all life on the planet.

6. The U.S. House of Representatives' Committee on Science, Space, and Technology is bringing charges against the lead signatory of the above letter because he posted the information letter on the public website of his research group, which is funded by the U.S. government, without permission.

Given these observations and stories, how can educators help students make sense of climate change? Below, I carefully sequence a unit addressing that question and leading students toward scientific literacy.

## UNIT GOALS

The primary goal of this unit is to scaffold and purposefully sequence tasks for science students that support their scientific understanding—that is, their science literacy. In doing so, it's imperative to immerse students in situations and provide tasks for them to engage a science topic, make sense of relevant data, and communicate their findings to others. This sequence, in turn, invokes opportunities for scientific argumentation. Students are asked to reach consensus through a process known as argument-driven inquiry (ADI) (Golden, Grooms, Sampson, & Oliveri, 2012; Sampson, Grooms, & Walker, 2011).

## ACTIVATING STUDENTS' PRIOR KNOWLEDGE

I begin this unit by asking the students what they already know and understand about the subject, what they've heard from others, what they've seen in the news and pop culture, and any other sources of information they may access. It helps me assess where to begin and to teach them where they are, as opposed to assuming they are blank slates for me to fill with my own thoughts and knowledge. I do tell the class the topic we are going to use is perceived by some to be controversial, but that we will focus only on scientific evidence about it to learn about forming scientific conclusions, not opinions. This introduction offers students guidelines and also our explicit learning goal, while also creating an opportunity for them to generate sincere questions about climate change regardless of most political perspectives.

## LEARNING TARGETS

As we move forward and keep discussions based on scientific evidence only, I place students in groups of three or four. Each group gets four or five of the following questions to explore and discuss: What do you know about global warming or climate change? Is the Earth's climate changing? What factors might cause the Earth's temperature to increase? What do scientists say about climate change today? How have scientists worked together to reach agreement about this issue? How can anyone use scientific data to identify facts about the world?

Students collaborate to answer these questions first, a few minutes apiece. These sincere questions invite them to talk in nonthreatening ways because the talk happens in small groups rather than at a whole-class or public level. Students simply share their understandings as primary knowers. They write their group answers on a whiteboard, and each group then reports, after practicing, to the whole class on what they discussed. As teacher, I'm able to formatively assess initial understandings, levels of consensus, possible misconceptions, and whether/how to move on to the next logical step in my plan. Subtle differences may become important later, and I tell students this unit is designed to help them learn how to answer scientific questions by analyzing the same evidence climate scientists use in their professional work.

## COGNITIVE LEARNING TARGETS

The targets for this lesson are as follows, and help me sequence tasks so they are logical and supportive of my students' learning:

1. Explore and analyze data about global climate change across multiple scientific sources.
2. Identify and evaluate patterns in the data about global climate change to determine possible causes and effects of global warming.
3. Compare prominent scientific hypotheses about climate change and explain them to practice scientific literacy.
4. Analyze arguments about climate change to evaluate differences between fact and opinion in science.

## FORMATIVE LEARNING TASK SEQUENCING

Because it is critical to the science of climate change, we model the concept and phenomenon of the greenhouse effect. The students, in pairs, create

Figure 7.1. Temperature Graph of Model "Earths"

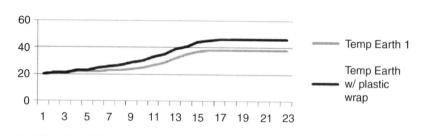

two model "Earths." Each Earth is a 2-liter bottle containing dirt and a thermometer. "Earth 1" is unwrapped, while "Earth 2" has plastic wrap on it to cause/simulate the green-house effect. Student pairs place their models equidistant from a light bulb (the "sun") and heat them for 15 minutes, recording temperature data for each Earth every 30 seconds. While students record data, I emphasize we are engaged in scientific modeling. As such, the sun is modeled by the bulb, Earth 1 models the atmosphere when greenhouse effects are absent, and Earth 2 is modeled by the bottle with plastic wrap to model greenhouse effect gas production in the atmosphere. When they are done collecting data, students construct a time/temperature graph with two lines on it to represent each Earth model. The graph will likely look like Figure 7.1.

As seen in Figure 7.1, the temperature increases in each model, then levels off to an equilibrium temperature. However, the temperature of Earth 1 increases more, and most students infer that is due to applying the greenhouse effect to it. They complete graphs and discuss their findings, while I explain the term *equilibrium temperature* and make it explicit that what they have just done is develop a scientific model they can use to test ideas and answer questions in science. Being scientific but still a model means it's accurate in some ways and inaccurate in others. For example, it is inaccurate in that the Earth is not wrapped in plastic like our bottles, those bottles are not made from the same material as the Earth's atmosphere, and of course the sun isn't that close to the Earth ("Feel the burn!"). The plastic wrap *artificially* captures hot air and forces it to stay in the bottle, while actual greenhouse gas does not. Rather, it captures *re-radiated* heat, not hot air, and keeps it within the atmosphere.

Students then compare their models and data. It is important to point out here that all of science uses conceptual models like this. It's also critical to point out that the greenhouse effect, only modeled here, is actually a *natural* effect. Scientists arguing that global warming is changing our climate cite data they conclude show that humans are *adding* greenhouse gases and accelerating the naturally occurring greenhouse effect in ways that may cause climate change.

**Figure 7.2.** **Global Temperature Changes: Last ~130 Years**

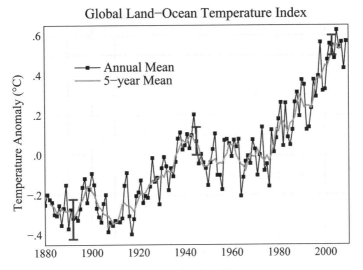

Global Land–Ocean Temperature Index

*Source:* http://data.giss.nasa.gov/gistemp/graphs_v3/

Once students have engaged the modeling tasks above, we turn to analyzing actual climate science data. I instruct students that now their task is to review data to determine any patterns they can detect (e.g., cooling patterns, warming patterns, sea levels, weather patterns, etc.). I then place students in groups of three or four and give them data sets as shown in Figures 7.2 and 7.3.

From Figure 7.2, students can infer several scientific facts: The Earth's average temperature shows a pattern of increase overall, the temperature varies sometimes, and each year is not necessarily hotter than the previous year. Students usually need help making sense of "temperature anomaly," that is, that a positive sign indicates temperatures being hotter than the average. Using Figure 7.3, students can infer that temperature and $CO_2$ are closely linked over time, that there are natural (not human-made) patterns of climate change every 100,000 years or so, that the planet has had periods of cooling as well as warming, and that current levels of $CO_2$ are higher than ever before in recorded history. We then analyze yet another graphic data set (see Figure 7.4).

Using the graphs in this sequence enables students to identify and discuss more and more evidence related to our topic of climate change. For example, with Figure 7.4 they learn that the mass of key glaciers has been decreasing (they've melted), but the total *number* of glaciers has increased. Using Figure 7.5 next, students further learn that Arctic Sea ice shows a pattern of decrease, Antarctic Sea ice shows slight increase, and the difference between the two poles is dramatic.

## Figure 7.3. Temperature and CO₂ Changes: Last 300,000 Years

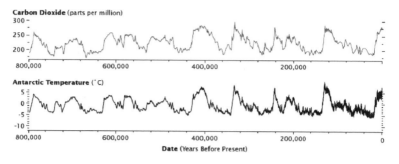

*Source:* www. nasa.gov

## Figure 7.4. Average Cumulative Mass Balance of "Reference" Glaciers Worldwide, 1945–2014

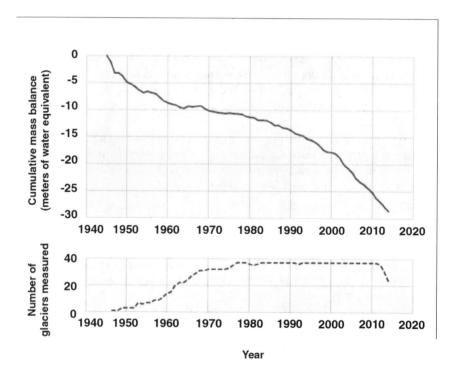

*Source:* www.epa.gov

**Figure 7.5. Arctic Sea Ice Extent at Minimum Months**

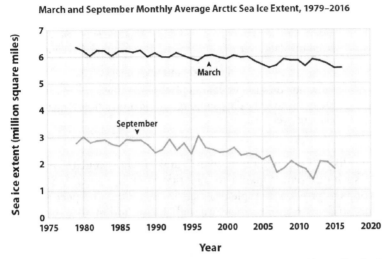

March and September Monthly Average Arctic Sea Ice Extent, 1979–2016

*Source:* NSIDC (National Snow and Ice Data Center), 2016. nsidc.org/data/seaice_index/archives.html. For more information, visit www.eps.gov/climatechange/indicators

With all these data presented in purposeful sequence, students next spend 5–10 minutes in groups interpreting and discussing the data. Then they collaborate to reach consensus and write their scientific findings and conclusions on a whiteboard in a format similar to that in Figure 7.6 (Golden et al., 2012).

As the students write their claims and arguments on the whiteboard, I make sure everyone in the group gives input. In general, the graphic organizer above helps students present patterns they found and explain how they used the data presented in class to support their findings. I emphasize it's important to get their thoughts written down and make sure their arguments are squarely evidence-based only. As they do this, I encourage them by asking questions such as, "What evidence supports this?" and "Is there any evidence to refute that?"

Once they finish these data interpretation tasks, each group elects a presenter for a round-robin class discussion. Each presenter's task is to explain the group's findings and evidence. I encourage them to elaborate beyond what they wrote down, to make guesses (hypotheses) and ask questions that can be tested or used to generate more data. Each group acts as audience members for another group's scientific presentation. Presenters take 5 minutes to explain and to field questions, and I emphasize the importance of students actively listening, asking questions, and *politely* pointing out inconsistencies. This is especially important if they hear arguments that are not evidence-based. It is common to hear students say things like, "It's warming," and for those listening to agree. To help them think more deeply, I ask prob-

**Figure 7.6. Whiteboard Format for ADI-Based Argumentation**

| Group members | Goal of investigation:<br>What climate patterns did you find? What facts can you infer from the data over time? (Is the Earth warming? Cooling? Etc.) |
|---|---|
| Explanation (What patterns do you see in the data?) | Evidence and reasoning:<br>How do you support your explanation of the data's meanings? Describe how the data support your identifications of patterns in climate over time. |

ing questions like, "Over what time span?" and "By how much?" to demonstrate how such differences matter to scientific meaning. After 5–8 minutes, I rotate groups to provide multiple practice opportunities and peer feedback. When done, students return to their original groups and modify their explanations based on any facts they gained from listening to their peers.

The round-robin format serves as a kind of "scientific peer review" that scientists also use to make meaning. Like scientists, students collect and review data, explain them, and communicate their understandings to peers for feedback and generation of new questions for further data collection and learning. That is, they engage in the literate practices of scientists.

As in teaching on purpose, sincere questions matter in scientific study. So does communicating findings in careful ways and with open minds. Our scientific touchstone is, "How do we know?"

All of the data presented are consistent with the idea that the Earth recently has been warming. The paleoclimate graph also shows that warming has happened in the past, so it is important to next ask the question: What is the most likely *cause* of current warming? At this point I explain it's important to infer possible causes of current warming from their data. To do that, we explore the two most common current explanations in climate science. These alternative explanations are described in Figure 7.7.

Two explanations are offered. The first currently is invoked by NASA, the National Oceanic and Atmospheric Administration, and the global scientific community: that recent warming, as one manifestation of climate change, is caused by carbon dioxide that humanity adds to the atmosphere, changing natural cycles. The alternative explanation, offered by others, is that the sun is the cause and sunspot activity better explains the phenomena in our data.

Now the students need even more data to address the causal explanations above. Figures 7.8–7.10 supply what students need.

Students again take 10–15 minutes to review and make sense of the new data in groups. They again write their findings on the whiteboard using the same format, with the exception that this time the goal is to explain the *causes* of warming rather than identify patterns. We review previous

**Figure 7.7. Explanations for Recent Warming**

| The Greenhouse Effect | Sunspots |
|---|---|
| The greenhouse effect is a phenomenon that occurs naturally, as some of the sun's energy is re-radiated by the Earth and is absorbed by gases in the Earth's atmosphere. These gases are called greenhouse gases (GHGs). Scientists like Fourier have long understood that GHGs cause an increase in the Earth's temperature. Many have long claimed that humanity is causing more GHGs, especially $CO_2$, to be captured in the atmosphere. This added $CO_2$ is thought to result in a higher temperature than would occur normally (an enhanced greenhouse effect). Some of the data below are relevant to this model. | Sunspots are sections of the sun's outer layer that appear to be dark in many photographs. Sunspots are known to go in cycles that occur on average every 11 years. Sunspots often have been associated with increased magnetic activity. Some have claimed that it is these increases in sunspot activity that best explain recent changes in the Earth's temperature. The graph in Figure 7.10 corresponds to sunspots (line). |

**Figure 7.8. Carbon Dioxide Levels in the Atmosphere (AKA the Keeling Curve)**

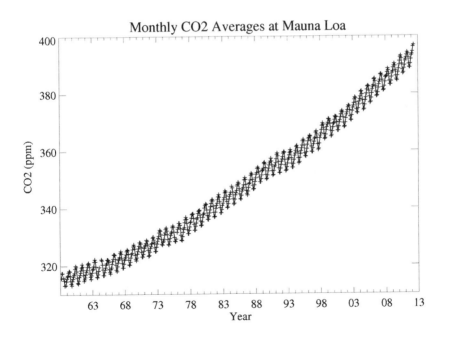

**Figure 7.9. Fossil Fuel Carbon Dioxide Emissions, 1880–2010**

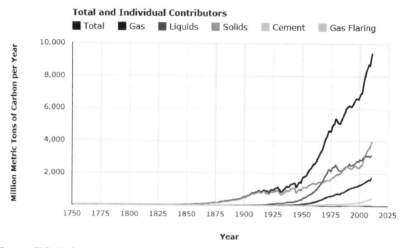

*Source:* T.G. Boden, G. Marland, & R.J. Andres. (2015). Global, regional, and national fossil fuel CO2 emissions. Carbon Dioxide Information Analysis Center. Oak Ridge National Laboratory, U.S. Department of Energy, Oak Ridge, TN. doi: 10.3334/CDIAC/00001_V2015

graphic data as well, especially Figure 7.3. Once again, when they have their arguments ready, they practice in a round-robin format requiring them to use only the data at hand. Some questions I strategically raise at this stage include: "How consistent are the data with the idea that humans cause warming through carbon dioxide emissions?" "How consistent are the data with the sunspot hypothesis?" and "As a scientist, what can you legitimately conclude from the data we've analyzed about climate change?"

After engaging in the second round-robin, I ask students to reach consensus: As scientists, what can they know based on the data? I stress the importance of this consensus and ask them whether they think scientists themselves agree overall on this topic or whether there is still debate. If there is still debate, then why? We discuss the implications of scientific consensus in relation to the identification of facts and the creation of new knowledge, and also take care to discuss the nature of scientific consensus. In the case of this topic, we do note that some scientists disagree and offer other findings and data, but that over 90% of scientists agree overall that their findings are consistent. This is important for two key reasons. First, it is important for science students to learn that scientific knowledge is rarely if ever total or static. Scientific knowledge, theories, and hypotheses about how the world works are constantly updated and revised depending on findings about new data, and part of the work of any scientist is to consistently check to confirm that known facts remain stable. More important for the purposes of engaging diverse learners as primary knowers in science, it is essential to allow space for disagreement and even dissent. Just as some scientists do not agree

**Figure 7.10. Solar Radiance**

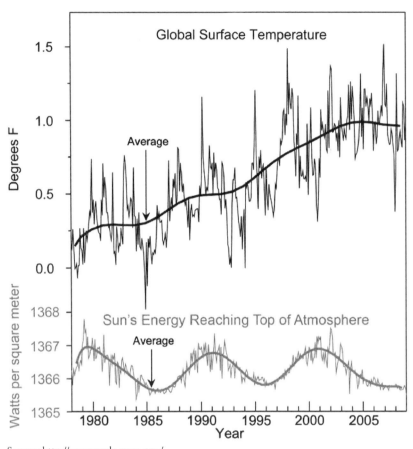

*Source:* http://www.ngdc.noaa.gov/

with their peers based on data, students must be provided the opportunities to engage in productive disagreement. Doing so leads to further inquiry for all students, requires both the learners and their teachers to maintain a scientific mindset for analyzing and understanding data, and more fully engages and promotes the value of divergent student responses during classroom work and learning.

For their summative task, I distribute statements made by relevant scientists/scientific organizations, and assign the students to review them, evaluate them in relation to prior data and findings, and then write an argument in which they explain not only their conclusions about climate change data, but also the nature of science as a way of thinking and learning about the world: How do scientists ask questions? How do they answer them?

When and how does scientific data become "fact" and "knowledge" about our world? Why is scientific consensus important? Their responses to these questions ensure that they don't just argue about global warming. They *use* that topic to learn how science works. They become science literate because I sequence this unit purposefully toward that target.

## SUMMATIVE ASSESSMENT AND CONCLUSION

After they turn in their individually written argumentative essays, I engage the entire class in discussion about what the scientific community thinks compared with them. I coach them to restrict themselves to data-based arguments and not political opinions, not because politics doesn't matter but because good scientists strive to think beyond political motives. Usually, a class comes to a consensus fairly similar to that of the global scientific community. If so, I emphasize that. If they conclude otherwise, I do *not* chastise them. To do so would be unresponsive as a teacher and defeat my purpose. Being a good scientist doesn't just mean knowing the facts and being "right" all the time. Good scientists actually require strong understandings of things like bias, scope, how theories work, and yes—even and especially failure. So I don't chastise students if they don't reach the same consensus as actual scientists. Instead, I realize what my next purpose must be: To continue designing tasks that help my students learn even more about how science and scientific literacy work. I embrace that purpose, and I respond.

# CHAPTER 8

# Asking Sincere Questions

Thus far we have been explaining what we mean by "responsive teaching." It means being responsive in two main senses: We respond to students' needs, and we also respond to meet standards that define instructional outcomes and inform disciplinary curricula. In this chapter we move into an essential but, for many teachers, elusive aspect of teaching: eliciting student engagement and helping students position themselves so they can evoke responses themselves by using sincere questions that are purposeful and meaningful. Much of education focuses on answers—in particular, getting the *right* answers, whatever they are supposed to be in a given situation and often as interpreted and determined by their teacher. Students are obsessed with being right. Teachers reward them for it. Tests do, too, and are designed so the number of correct answers defines intelligence and rewards it with the label of "success."

Giving "right" answers is privileged so much that as a goal it can make it hard for teachers to formulate queries truly worth asking for any reason besides "being right." This imbalance is somewhat based on time constraints of schooling, because checking right/wrong answers as matters of test performance is quicker than assessing the worth of the divergent responses we know students routinely should explore as matters for life. No Scantron machine can handle questions that allow multiple valid responses, so those questions often don't get asked. Their loss—or abandonment in the face of testing—is a good example of how purpose and meaning get lost in classrooms. When we ask questions to which there is only one answer, we lose opportunities to help students think in healthy and sophisticated ways.

We also lose opportunities when we don't help students to feel safe asking questions, as well as when we don't stay closely tuned when they answer our questions with "I don't know," which means that they either don't understand or aren't engaged, both circumstances requiring our attention. The popular saying that "there is no such thing as a stupid question" remains true. Vaunted scholar Carl Sagan (2011) wrote in defense of naïve questions and answers, stating that "every question is a cry to understand the world" (p. 303). Questions and the responses they evoke in a learning community are necessary in any academic endeavor. Certainly if you have ever written a thesis or been in an intellectual discussion, you noticed how difficult it is to ask a good, deep question well. Good questions require listening, inquiry, thought, and reflection by both the asker and the asked. Answering can be a quick affair, a simple yes/no, or an "I don't know." When questions are not carefully designed, students quickly learn that a lucky guess sometimes does just as well as an informed response. But no matter how students are questioned for understanding, it is clear that their abilities to provide a "correct" answer are much more valued compared with their abilities to think through alternatives and reason to understand a variety of potentially divergent but legitimate responses. The premium is on giving *right* answers, not asking the *best* questions, even though it is generally good questions that lead to powerful insights, realizations, innovations, and breakthroughs, whereas fixating on the *right* answers can and does frequently prevent students and teachers from fully engaging the potentials of their work together.

Asking a good, substantive question is the starting point for learning and can provide all the motivation needed to embark on learning tasks. In this chapter, we make the case that formulating, modeling, and promoting techniques for questioning are integral to teaching and learning, for a number of reasons. Questioning is active, a way to involve students as co-learners with us in our classrooms. Questions drive curiosity and motivation. They focus attention on texts, ideas, and objects. They very well may be the most important aspect of any learning episode.

## PLAYING GOTCHA

Pop quiz!

1. What is the function of endoplasmic reticulum in cell biology?
2. What are the steps of cell division, and how are mitosis and meiosis different?
3. What is a Punnet Square, and what is it used for?
4. What does the abbreviation "DNA" stand for?

These are some common, basic knowledge- and comprehension-level questions we might ask our students in a discussion, a quiz, or a test in a biology classroom. They are all concrete, recall questions that have concrete correct answers and no room for debate or variation. Such factual questions can easily be Googled online today to find their answers, and although they are important facts for classroom participants to use in abstract conversations about the texts they study and the topics they read and write about, many can be answered without developing any deep comprehension of the content. Why engage in real learning when you can just look up the answers with a smartphone?

There is also something fishy about single-answer questions in general, and most of our students immediately smell the problem. *Their teach-*

*ers already know all the answers.* Give the teacher the answer she expects and move on. These fact-based, low-level questions tell students that we, as teachers, know more than they do, that we put a premium on certain answers and not others, and that we have everything figured out already as we wait to see whether they can figure it out too. They position students to be receivers of knowledge, not active partners in the process of their own learning. "Just the facts"-style questions tell them the world is something to memorize and regurgitate in short-answer format when they are called upon in school. These smaller questions unintentionally signal to our students that everything worth knowing is already known and that there is nothing new under the sun, let alone anything worth talking about: Just pay attention and you will learn. It's magic!

Small questions indicate for students that knowledge is important but external to them, shutting their views, identities, and perspectives out of their own learning processes. These questions kill curiosity and turn off students. They shut many out of class discussions because if they are ignorant, then they cannot (and will not) risk participating, and if they are already *right*, they have very little motivation to engage further. Why answer questions the teacher already has the answers to? It's like playing "gotcha." And then it seems like they will never need these answers again.

Despite spitting out question after question, such atomized and fixed approaches to classroom interaction may center on less concrete kinds of knowledge that do not really connect meaningfully with factual details in a content-area lesson or unit of instruction. For example, the way literature often gets discussed in English classes ends with things tied up in tidy bows even though most literary theories highlight that all texts contain huge amounts of potential meaning in relation to things learners say, read, write, and do. Depending on context, responses and meaning can change or allow for multiple appropriate answers or methods of answering. Using Punnet Squares in biology class, teachers can ask questions all day about how and why different genetic combinations of dominant and recessive traits result in different results. But teaching this way becomes like following a set of IKEA instructions written to help assemble a bookshelf, with specific steps leading to specific, unchanging outcomes that may or may not result in one putting the pieces together backward. Slavish devotion to fact-based questions as *the* vehicles for instruction ignores the vital, interesting, and compelling aspects of truly engaging learning and classroom work. When the teacher already has answers to all the questions, the class takes on a monologue format for most students—a dreaded lecture rather than a lively collaborative experience. Intended or not, instruction using nothing but recall questions becomes a process for teachers to deliver information and students to receive it, no questions asked. That's a bit ironic, don't you think?

Certainly, recall/knowledge/comprehension questions are necessary; concrete facts are required for basic comprehension. And teachers *should* share their experiences and knowledge with their pupils. Some parts of that work require asking single-solution questions because facts are important. However, these moments should be seen as formative and not central to learning tasks. When such narrow activity is the only recourse for teachers and students, it shuts off conversation. Because conversation is a proven collaborative strategy that increases student learning and engagement; asking questions that shut it down is unhealthy. It not only shifts purpose away from students' needs, but violates and reduces what we know is required for success. Students' thoughts, views, opinions, concerns, and identities—their prior knowledge as primary knowers—become at best secondary, and at worst devalued and dismissed, during class. Their voices are not considered, and they do not have the opportunity to discuss what they feel is important, relevant, or vital. It then becomes easier for students to dismiss instruction, and easier to think schoolwork is just busywork rather than something to value in their everyday lives and futures. In this shallow format, students have few opportunities to formulate their own thoughts, opinions, and questions. They have little to do except observe, take notes, and memorize according to the teacher's commands. They are prepared to parrot the teacher, not make meaning for themselves. They become sycophants and yes-men who do not engage with texts and accept whatever they are told is true or right. They go through the motions and bide their time until they graduate. Or, worse, they fail to follow, struggle, fail, quit trying, and maybe even drop out. Even teachers find asking the same ham-handed questions all day creates a grinding, even soul-killing spectacle of their work, whereas they dreamed of setting students' minds on fire with big questions about life, people, and how the world works.

Instead of getting lost in the triage of covering textbooks and preparing for tests that require "just the facts," teachers can design and promote rich dialogues where students practice thinking and action. After all, that is what will be expected of them once they complete their academic apprenticeships and become adults. Below, we detail three considerations for formulating questions and planning instruction, combining question formats espoused by prior researchers and educators (Harvey, 2002; Perkins, 1995; Wiggins & McTighe, 2005). Teachers should purposely design big, meaningful questions about ideas and topics that matter to students and use those big questions to drive all instruction.

These questions need to be *sincere*. They need to *connect* texts, subjects, and content areas. They also need to be *relevant*, bridging students' in- and out-of-school lives. By relevant, we mean useful and meaningful to the students—not because we teachers think our students *ought* to value what we teach, but because we have analyzed our students' identities and knowledge to collect data that enable us to *know* what they value and to use that to ask them questions in ways that excite them to answer. Sincere questions may start in classrooms, but the best questions open students up to what lies beyond school and lead to greater understandings in and of the world.

## SINCERE QUESTIONS

Questions should have their origins in real student thoughts and concerns. They should be what Harvey (2002) calls "sincere questions," driven by students' curiosity. Young children are not shy about asking many questions, like "Why don't the Three Bears lock their doors?" "Why is the sky blue?" or "How do you know the refrigerator light really goes off when you close the door?" They are curious and concerned about lots of things, but in school many teachers treat students' curiosities as distractions from the curriculum and "real learning," instead of considering how to use those genuine questions to design instruction that will excite students by making them feel smart, capable, and valued. This often is especially true as students get older. Teachers and parents take less time addressing what older students *want* to know and more time teaching what they feel students *ought* to know. For the record, those *oughts* need to be taught, to some degree, but they become unhealthy when they become the center of what we do. We *can* and *should* frame those very same questions students ask and make them the fodder for a great many desirable and interesting learning tasks, opportunities for student inquiry, and fun discussions that connect students' academic work explicitly with their lives in general. Basic questions can be corralled, repurposed, and used to guide instruction in any unit if teachers can revise them in ways that are connected and responsive to their specific students' needs and goals at a specific time. Sincere questions make those connections obvious and explicit.

Scholars have wrestled with multiple contentious questions over the years, and although we are not deluded enough to think all our students will go on to spend their days inquiring into the mysteries of the universe 24/7, there are many avenues for evoking lively, relevant, thoughtful conversations about texts and topics we teach across all subjects. Many texts we teach contain ambiguities or strange juxtapositions that beg to be discussed, and they do not always lead to clean conclusions. The most productive questions allow divergent answers—answers that differ and lead to variable conclusions, many of which are appropriate, valid, and evidence-based at the same time. Sometimes we cannot predict where responses to sincere questions will take us, a condition that Fecho and Amatucci (2008) wrote can feel like "spinning out of control" (p. 5). However, we need to risk spinning with our students sometimes and use all the resources available to us as professionals to invite and attract students into discussions of reading, writing, and thinking about the world, no matter what subject is labeled on the schedule. It sometimes may be uncomfortable for teachers or students to engage in such circumstances, especially if they lack experience and practice. We must remember that there are rarely definitive answers to truly sincere questions, and that some people seek definite resolution of these matters and must be helped to learn to be comfortable with ambiguity. But it is the sincere, open, divergent questions that don't have set answers that are most generative for our students and ourselves. Sincere questions are productive and essential to explore over time with all learners.

Many of us seek tidy endings and set quantities in our content areas. Western models of teaching remain largely unchanged from the one described by Aristotle. From those perspectives, all teaching should end with resolution in learning. Not all of these resolutions need be happy. For example, in English literature we know students will soon discover that everyone in Elsinore Castle may be dead, but we know how it turns out. That's a resolution that results when teachers ask basic questions about a text. But clear purpose and meaning are not a given beyond that. Students might realize *Hamlet* ends in tragedy without making much sense of what that means or why they should care, unless we ask them sincere questions and help them connect with that drama's topics and themes. Just as there is no uniform way to teach every class or to address every single student's needs, there are also many questions that have multiple possible responses: Is *Huckleberry Finn* a racist text? What is the most appropriate function to use when solving a mathematical problem? How is history made? How did life on the Earth happen? The answers to these questions are manifold and contingent, and they offer chances for students to combine their impressions and experiences productively for learning via the tasks we design.

Sincere questions as described above offer multiple, ongoing chances for students to respond, consider approaches they might need to understand, think about alternative interpretations or surprising implications, and write about texts and ideas in ways that connect what they learn in school to what they know, live, and value in life. Open-ended questions fuel motivation in two senses. First, they do not have simple, pat answers. Answering them requires students to reason and engage in learning tasks, and to use evidence and logic to explain understandings when there is wiggle room for interpretation, and it helps students see new ways to make connections between what they are learning and other things they know and do already. Second, sincere questions offer multiple avenues for inquiry so students can provide reasonable evidence for their responses and justify them. The teacher can then use responses as additional formative data that help in deciding what to ask or do next, and in making learning far more interactive and engaging than it is in environments where interaction is more or less laminated and limited by the format of (1) teacher asks question with known answer, (2) student answers, and (3) teacher responds with feedback about whether the student was correct. Students become tentative when they risk revealing ignorance in ways that can be heard as "wrong" or "stupid" by peers or teachers (Hall, Burns, & Greene, 2013). The stakes are high for them when being wrong means being embarrassed. Offering different types of responses with a teacher who helps refine their explorations and answers to sincere questions can be quite liberating, especially when the point is not to be right or wrong but to collaboratively practice using the evidence, facts, reasoning, and applications to do useful things. There are no unitary right answers in learning tasks founded on sincere questions. Instead of answers, there is learning.

## GENERATIVE QUESTIONS

Sincere questions should be generative, taking a cue from the Teaching for Understanding model partly developed by David Perkins (1995) at Harvard University. Such generative questions have the following five features:

- They are central to one or more disciplines or domains.
- They are interesting to students.
- They are accessible to students (there are lots of resources available to help students pursue the topic).
- They have multiple connections to students' experiences both in and out of school.
- And, perhaps most important, they are interesting to the teacher. (Fusaro, 2008).

Questions designed this way promote interdisciplinary learning. Government treatises, research reports, science articles, news accounts, legal documents, persuasive essays, fictional narratives, and documentaries are not just the provinces of one content area, in this way of thinking. Reading, writing, and thinking span tasks and content areas, promoting purposeful teaching in which learning and skills are not atomized, isolated, and reduced to emptiness and rote memorization without meaning.

The literal definition of curriculum is "the subjects comprising a course of study in a school or college." Subjects, you'll note, is plural. Too often, because of how middle and high schools have been managed in U.S. public education, chasms have opened between the content areas. These fracture points are well defended and maintained in most secondary schools, but it would be best if those boundaries were relaxed so students could get a better conception of the world. After all, would it not help to know about biology and physics when reading a novel like *Frankenstein*? Alternatively, if you were teaching genetics in a biology class, wouldn't it be interesting to talk about how people explored the nature of life, while students read a gothic horror novel in which the author depicted the dangers of "playing God"? Would it not help if you had a working knowledge of statistics when reading a politician's reasons for proposing a law, and wouldn't it be more fulfilling if the policies and statistics studied in government were about issues and topics students were already curious to know about? Would it not be in our students' interests to know some chemistry before they actually drank the latest delicious energy drink that might kill them due to toxicity? Wouldn't it be fun to think about how advertising made you feel like you *needed* the latest wonder product everyone else was getting because the infomercial for it was just too cool to ignore? These are all questions that, used strategically, can help teachers build instruction around sincere questions about topics their students then want to learn about as a result.

Generative, sincere questions are doubly useful. They drive planning for the teacher *and* provide opportunities for students to ask their own additional sincere questions and inquire beyond that design. Having sincere questions in mind provides a thread throughout any instructional unit and makes instruction more coherent and relevant. It takes the guesswork out of class and gives students clear reasons to participate. Schools are places where students too often have no say in basic matters of their own lives, like walking in hallways or going to the bathroom or even being allowed to speak. They require reasons to do what teachers ask of them, and that's a reasonable expectation. Using sincere, intriguing, generative questions that interest them goes a long way toward meeting that expectation.

Schools are places where students do not have much choice. They don't get to choose most of the classes they take, they don't choose when they get tested, and they don't choose when they meet and work. This situation can be addressed in part by asking rich questions that help them to explore topics and generate their own questions, then complete tasks such as keeping what Harvey (2002) calls a wonder journal where students use those questions and class responses as springboards for their own genuine questions about what they study. These questions directly relate to subject area content. They also reveal common misconceptions or prior knowledge about the topic, but instead of doing so in the antiseptic environment of traditional "school," these questions generate lively environments with a spirit of collaboration in response to students' own identities as people. Sincere questions elicit information about what students already know and what their strengths are, both of which are essential data sets for success in responsive teaching. They also provide insight into what students really learn and want to learn, and provide teachers with additional questions to frame unit plans over time with continuity and coherence that increase success.

## ESSENTIAL QUESTIONS

Students go to school to become informed citizens, and that means schools must offer opportunities for them to appreciate literature and arts, use logic, solve problems, and understand social systems. The real world doesn't separate these concerns by content area, and we do students a disservice if we don't at least offer chances to consider, act, and question under similar conglomerate circumstances. Certainly, the specifics of content-area learning will encourage the development and answering of questions, and the ability to use different knowledge bases together can lead to more sophisticated understandings of how school subjects work together to help students become educated adults.

Some questions go beyond specific content areas, though, to address the many nebulous concerns of real life. Wiggins and McTighe (2005) refer to these kinds of questions as *essential* questions in their Understanding by Design model, and their conception is similar to our idea of *sincere* questions. Essential questions are topical and overarching. They go across texts, promoting connections between the study of texts and understanding of the world. They are big questions about life, the world, and people's places in society. Essential questions are not just matters of philosophy, or navel gazing with no real point. They provide lenses for examination and thought about academic concepts, skills, and practices. They provide opportunity for critical and higher order thinking like analysis (breaking things down to understand how they work), synthesis (putting parts together in new ways to understand their use), and evaluation (making judgments about whether, how, and why something has value). Essential questions motivate and engage students in instruction because they are immediately relevant and interesting. That is, they are *sincere*. They're real, not "gotchas"! They're invitations.

Perhaps the most useful effect of essential, sincere questions is they can be asked, examined, and re-examined many times without losing relevance over time. Questions like "Why do people hurt one another?" "What makes relationships work?" or "What does it mean to be different?" are excellent starting points for talking about many topics, texts, historical events, scientific phenomena, and other school topics. They are not tied to any text, but can be used purposefully with many texts to help students engage on their terms in ways proven to increase learning. These are the questions that drive instruction, and are the foci of the various instructional unit models we include throughout this book.

## CONCLUSION

Our considerations about questions are not meant to be touchy-feely, portraying a stereotypical teacher who wants students to talk constantly about their feelings and thoughts without regard to evidence or facts. We do not advocate approaches where every answer is equally right. The key to successful questioning is to frame questions so students can *use* them with one another to interact in new ways and do things with new ideas in order to respond. The best way to learn is to do. Students need time and opportunities to practice reading and writing, and over-emphasis on factual information based on dead-end questions only reinforces a notion that they don't have to do anything but regurgitate in order to succeed. A balance wherein academic content and students' prior knowledge intertwine with the teacher's responsive and purposely designed instruction is the professional way. Expert teachers ask questions that motivate students to think and respond of their own volition, not because answering earns a good grade or a piece of candy for agreeing to join in.

We do our students a disservice when we promote the idea that important questions are those that have a single answer. When we allow ourselves to take that easier way, we teach students to seek simple solutions, see nothing but pat responses, and engage in thoughtless actions that are fruitless even when they might seem like fun *activities*. Activity simply means doing stuff, whereas we recommend purposeful *learning tasks* that require doing meaningful work. The point of education across all content areas is to open up and examine the multiplicity of the world through reading, writing, speaking, listening, and otherwise communicating in as many ways as possible about academic knowledge and how to use it in life. Narrowing schoolwork down to simplistic routines and rote activities that give the illusion of doing something is a disconnection from reality no matter how fun we (and the students) think those activities might be. "Activities" are not inherently bad, but teachers must constantly ask whether they are extensions of deliberate learning tasks that help students meet clearly useful goals. If we don't connect our teaching to students' realities, we ignore the fact that they are in our rooms to learn how to face multiple situations and navigate them with no easy answers and no pat solutions. Simple recall or concrete questions are important, but they are limiting when we use them unmindfully as focal points in lessons and units. They support comprehension and scaffold student experiences with new ideas, but if they become the center and end rather than merely the means to learning, they become prohibitive. Put differently, Forest Gump required leg braces to walk, but they were in his way when he needed to run. Good teachers know that asking sincere questions helps students kick up their feet and sprint faster than they ever dreamed toward their futures. When we do it on purpose, they'll never stop running. That's when we know we've succeeded. In the next chapter, we demonstrate purposeful use of questions in a social studies classroom.

# CHAPTER 9

# Model Unit Plan 3

## Using Sincere Questions to Teach Imperialism in Social Studies

*Ryan New,*
*Boyle County High School, Danville, Kentucky*

### INTRODUCTION

The concept (and ongoing phenomenon) of imperialism in global society offers students multiple sincere opportunities to explore themes that affect them locally and internationally—in much the same way as the Cold War and the War on Terror changed the worldviews of many people now reading this book, when they were young. During the end-of-the-year reflection, when students offer me feedback to help strengthen my instruction, a student commented in particular on this unit I designed about the concept and history of imperialism, saying, "I am still blown away by imperialism. How could we [the United States] have done those terrible things in the Philippines? How could racism possibly be an excuse? Why haven't we learned about this sooner?"

The last question that student asked is still my favorite, years later. It highlights that essential quality and real connection to the instruction I designed. Her comments and questions demonstrate precisely why we should study big topics like imperialism. Apart from discussing whether imperialism resulted in more harm than good, studying it as a fundamental historical phenomenon positions my students as primary knowers who can have rich, contemporary conversations about race, nationalism, the impact of technology, resource allocation, global trade, and a myriad of social and economic ideas that are all *connected* and *meaningful* beyond class (and beyond mere knowledge of facts).

By studying imperialism as a central concept that drives an entire unit of instruction, I purposely use history to help students understand how their own worlds work today (including how imperialism still operates all over the world). Imperialism, therefore, presents a conceptual platform from which students can explore social studies as a subject area and also consider the less pleasant aspects of history to reflect on what it means to be both a citizen and a human being.

The unit that follows, developed with the teaching on purpose approach to instructional design, can be adapted by readers to make it work for them however they need it to in order to succeed. While I teach the unit with honor students, the intrinsic importance and interest of the topic make it a good one to teach with students of all skill levels, with resources that still allow them to engage deeply with the content and issues.

When teaching on purpose, even something as simple as a sincere unit *title* can help students engage and learn more than just the topic for an instructional unit. In that vein, I do not offer a catchy title for this unit model —on purpose. This unit is titled "Imperialism" (and nothing more) for a reason. It is a powerful term in itself, one with many facets and examples, and I did not want to narrow it or diminish it with something catchy.

## UNIT TITLE: IMPERIALISM

### Context

Before I can start backward mapping (from standards to assessment to targets to tasks and back again), and before I can impart any historical thinking skills, I first must understand where my students have been and where they are going. This imperialism unit is part of a sophomore honors world civilization class that runs from the Renaissance to the Cold War. It's the students' first major exposure to modern, non-U.S. history at the secondary level so I can assume based on experience that most students have some familiarity with the major topics, such as the Renaissance, Industrial Revolution, World War I, Holocaust, and Nazis. But I also can assume they lack prior knowledge of the Reformation, the French Revolution, imperialism, and the Cold War. Of my 40 students, most are college bound and will use my instruction to position themselves to enter AP U.S. history and other advanced courses.

My students generally have little initial knowledge of imperialism, but that is actually an asset to learning in this case, and I intentionally use teacher-guided inquiry to help students to figure out on their own much of what imperialism is and how it manifests. Imperialism as a practice is heavy stuff to process. The representations usually elicit revulsion and anger. Many students simply struggle to believe it was possible for people to commit such violence, and they often are subsequently harsh in their judgment if I don't help mediate their academic dispositions. Historians talk a lot about presentism—the retrofitting of today's morals to critique the past—and unless we address that together, students' historical thinking skills are compromised and they reach only obvious conclusions, that is, "Imperialism was terrible, how could this have ever happened?" But that is precisely the point and question for study, and I make sure to elicit it at the beginning, not the end. Because the students have *heard* about imperialism, I know I can help them take a fresh crack at the topic and go deeper.

Working backward from where I want them to be, I design elements for inquiry, develop high, explicit expectations, and present the skills needed for independent learning at those rigorous levels. Key skills that are used in this unit and require instruction and practice as each is introduced, if they have not been taught previously, include the following, all of which are incorporated in the unit:

- Question Formulation Technique, or QFT—The Question Formulation Technique (Rothstein & Santana, 2011) is a process through which students learn to generate their own questions. The QFT offers a strong and structured process for developing sincere questions that help students focus on the importance of questions at deeper levels. The four rules are easy to implement at any point during a lesson:
  - » Ask as many questions as possible in the time provided.
  - » Do not pause to discuss responses or aspects of any questions to encourage student thinking and ability to think with and across multiple questions.
  - » Write and use each question specifically as it is written.
  - » Change any statements that arise into questions to increase amount of inquiry.
- Document Based Questions, or DBQs—Document Based Questions enable students to develop evidence-based claims (DBQ Project, 2015). DBQs help students analyze documents and then corroborate their claims to evoke a statement of argument or other thesis and support for it. While I break down a DBQ into its constituent parts at the beginning of the year, I finally get to an actual DBQ after midyear. Standard DBQ parts include:
  - » Topic of document to be analyzed
  - » Author's purpose for discussing the topic
  - » Historical context of the document
  - » Audience (whom is the document for and why?)
  - » Paideia Seminar—Paideia Seminars (Adler, 1998) are student-led discussions wherein the teacher plays almost no role in the talk. Intervening only to clarify major issues or include more students, the teacher listens while students discuss documents in the context of the unit and formatively tracks conversation on a participation sheet. Due to the demands on students' listening and communication skills, I also break this down into its constituent parts to allow students to acclimate:

* Specifying the text that will serve as the central source for student inquiry and discussion.
* Providing contextual background and details (author background, historical context, etc., as appropriate).
* Reviewing key vocabulary required for fully successful participation.
* Initiating seminar using opening questions that require consideration of main ideas and key concepts.
* Guiding students to explore core questions focused on analysis of the central source text.
* Guiding students to answer and note responses to closing questions that support critical thinking, analysis, and preparation for individual ongoing oral and written responses.

## Main Idea Development

We practice using the QFT on the first day of the unit and usually confirm through the questions that are developed that the students have rarely if ever explored this era in history. By asking sincere questions using QFT, students are better able to explore imperialism through systematic inquiry, a process that is guided yet is driven by students' interests and inquiries. Good inquiry must be planned for and guided in order for novices to gain fluency.

Students need to read multiple sources with divergent views, and those sources must be given equal treatment to ensure students see multiple and conflicting arguments. Teaching this unit as an inquiry project is more powerful when students don't know much about the topic while still beginning with high interest. The lack of prior experience/awareness motivates them to work, and requires me to be purposeful when selecting documents, assessments, and tasks. Some of the featured sources that I use with students include:

* Hochschild, A. (1998). *King Leopold's ghost: A story of greed, terror, and heroism in colonial Africa.* Boston, MA: Houghton Mifflin.
* Twain, M. (1992). *Collected tales, sketches, speeches, & essays, 1852–1890* (L. J. Budd, Ed.). New York, NY: Library of America.
* Orwell, G. (1981). *A collection of essays.* San Diego, CA: Harcourt Brace Jovanovich.
* Kipling, R. (1899). The White man's burden. Retrieved from public. wsu.edu/~brians/world_civ/worldcivreader/world_civ_reader_2/ kipling.html
* Morel, E. D. (1903). The Black man's burden. Retrieved from www.csun.edu/~jaa7021/hist434/Morel.pdf
* Spielvogel, J. J. (2009). *Western civilization.* Southbank, Victoria, Australia: Thomson Learning Australia.

The following sincere questions guide the planning and teaching of this unit:

1. *For the teacher*
   a. What do my students already know about imperialism?
   b. How can I use what students already know about in life to activate prior knowledge and make the topic relevant?
   c. How I can help students transition from analyzing documents for comprehension to making meaning from evidence derived from answering sincere questions about imperialism using the texts I selected for class?

2. *Teacher-derived for the students*
   a. What is imperialism? Does it still matter in today's world?
   b. How and why did mostly White, European populations conquer, colonize, and control non-White racial populations and foreign territories around the world between the 15th and 20th centuries?
   c. How did the Industrial Revolution influence imperialism, especially what some have labeled U.S. imperialism? How has the idea of U.S. imperialism affected our country and its relationships with other nations and groups around the world today?

## EXPLICIT LEARNING GOALS AND TARGETS: CONCEPTS, SKILLS, AND PRACTICES

My ultimate purpose in this unit was to design engaging learning tasks that enhanced students' writing ability and promoted historical thinking through inquiry within the context of imperialism as a concept in the discipline of history. I purposefully aligned the lessons to national social studies standards based on an inquiry approach with built-in writing support tasks, introduced documents for the students to categorize and use in response to document-based questions, built in deep tasks like simulations and Paideia Seminars centered around historical literature, built formative assessments that documented learning progress while enhancing writing skills, and created a summative assessment based on student-generated questions developed during formative tasks engaged during the unit. This summative assessment combined student-generated questions from the QFT and historical documents to create authentic DBQs for the class. My goal for students was to teach them to act as independent learners who could use inquiry skills and social studies concepts in everyday life. As such, my cognitive learning targets were as follows:

1. Students will analyze historical documents related to the topic of imperialism and categorize them.
2. Students will use evidence from historical documents about imperialism to evaluate historical events and interpret their meanings.
3. Students will use evidence-based interpretations of historical facts related to imperialism to make meaningful connections with current events in their own world(s).
4. Students will use evidence to interpret historical facts and answer questions related to historical documents about imperialism relevant to modern society.
5. Students will simulate imperialist acts, events, and concepts in order to evaluate and synthesize historical knowledge.
6. Students will discuss topics related to imperialism using Paideia discussion formats to evaluate and use historical thinking and conceptual knowledge from social studies in their lives beyond school.

## LESSON SEQUENCE

Teaching presents enough variables in a day-to-day setting, so planning with a summative assessment in mind is essential to giving students your full attention during this unit. You have to know what you expect students to do after instruction and practice, if you want to purposefully help them succeed at the highest rates possible. If you show them your plans and explain how the unit will proceed, students can see the progression of their tasks and become able to track their own progress, increasing their self-efficacy. To do this I provide students with a unit timeline that guides both them and me to keep a responsive and adaptive pace without subjecting them to "gotcha" questions, when they know every question in advance because we either talked about it or they generated it.

Included in the unit are the standards that explain lesson outcomes, daily topics for pacing, targets for learning, specific factual information (SFI) and terms needed to engage each lesson, and assignment due dates (Shick & Hierl, 2007). Anticipating the needs of my classes, I intentionally build in an extra 5 days per semester for extended time for enrichment based on student interest, spillover time, teachable moments, and inevitable interruptions that happen in all schools. As a result, and because I plan for it on purpose, my students are better able to manage their time in case of missed classes or future conflicts. These unit guides are, by far, the most intentional planning I do, and they serve as the backbone of my plans and assessments (see Figure 9.1). Abbreviations that appear in all my plans include:

- Notation for standards (e.g., D2.His. 3.9–12)
- QFT—Question Formulation Technique
- SFI—Specific factual information needed by students
- MI—Main idea, wherein students synthesize what they've read into a single-sentence main idea

I include the full unit plan in Figure 9.1 to provide an overview just as I would for students, but it becomes much clearer in the text that follows it.

This unit is bookended by student-generated questions and ends with students answering many of them. They use the Question Formulation Technique on images related to imperialism to expose their prior knowledge on the subject. Each lesson has a target that corresponds to either concept development or skill building, and these are kept distinct even as they are used in concert. Students analyze both secondary and primary documents, with my guidance, to better understand questions they ask (and are asked) at the beginning of the unit, but as part of a final review, students evaluate the goals and consequences of imperialism themselves. Formative assessments are not described in the unit plan, but are included via entrance and exit slips focused on daily writing practice for each lesson. Summative assessment entails a student-guided DBQ, wherein students use the questions they generated during the QFT and I give them documents to help support their answers. Students then create claims based on the evidence from historical documents.

Because I teach this unit using guided inquiry, the C3 Social Studies Framework (National Council for the Social Studies, 2013) provides an excellent set of standards that focus our inquiry cycle. These skills-based standards support student understanding by guiding them through developing questions, using historical thinking and geographical reasoning, collecting and using sources, and communicating evidence-based conclusions. This is the first unit in which my students engage the entirety of such an inquiry cycle.

## UNIT DESIGN: SCAFFOLDING READING, WRITING, AND SPEAKING INTO A COLLECTIVE UNDERSTANDING

This is what I call a "transitional unit," or a scaffolded unit, which is taught later in the year and in which I begin to provide extensive autonomy to the students. Prior to this unit, we look at individual documents in the context of the overall unit topic but within a classroom setting. In order to maximize time within this transitional unit, I adopt a flipped classroom approach wherein students study basic factual content at home, familiarize themselves with the documents, and then work in collaborative groups for the first half

Developing Compelling and Supporting Questions

- D1.4.9–12. Explain how supporting questions contribute to an inquiry and how, through engaging source work, new compelling and supporting questions emerge.

Disciplinary Concepts (Geography and History)

- D2.Geo.5.9–12. Evaluate how political and economic decisions throughout time have influenced cultural and environmental characteristics of various places and regions.
- D2.His.1.9–12. Evaluate how historical events and developments were shaped by unique circumstances of time and place as well as broader historical contexts.
- D2.His.3.9–12. Use questions generated about individuals and groups to assess how the significance of their actions changes over time and is shaped by the historical context.
- D2.His.5.9–12. Analyze how historical contexts shaped and continue to shape people's perspectives.
- D2.His.7.9–12. Explain how the perspectives of people in the present shape interpretations of the past.
- D2.His.14.9–12. Analyze multiple and complex causes and effects of events in the past.

Gathering, Evaluating, and Using Evidence

- D3.1.9–12. Gather relevant information from multiple sources representing a wide range of views while using the origin, authority, structure, context, and corroborative value of the sources to guide the selection.
- D3.3.9–12. Identify evidence that draws information directly and substantively from multiple sources to detect inconsistencies in evidence in order to revise or strengthen claims.

Communicating Conclusions

- D4.1.9–12. Construct arguments using precise and knowledgeable claims, with evidence from multiple sources, while acknowledging counterclaims and evidentiary weaknesses.

Lessons* N.B. May need extra days (1–2)

1. Imperialism QFT
   a. Target: I can create my own questions from images of imperialism
2. New Imperialism—Overview
   a. Target: I can explain the political, social, and economic causes of imperialism

**Figure 9.1. Continued**

    b. SFI: Imperialism, nationalism, imperial propagandists, Social Darwinist, racism, "White Man's Burden," quinine, machine gun, malaria, steamship, telegraph, humanitarian, missionary, Christianizing, rubber, oil, tin, Karl Marx, V.I. Lenin, exploitation

    c. **Assignment: MI—New Imperialism**

3. Scramble for Africa Simulation

    a. Target: I can analyze the role that Europe played in the Scramble for Africa from the point of view of both the Europeans and Africans

    b. SFI: Scramble for Africa

    c. **Assignment: MI—Scramble for Africa + Preparation for Simulation**

4. DBQ Africa 1

    a. Target: I can create corroborative evidence to create an argument for a DBQ

    b. SFI: Partition of Africa, *steam engine, *telegraph, *maxim gun, *repeating rifle (*how they were used in colonizing), examples of colonial resources (3–5), importation vs. exportation, Sub-Saharan

    c. **Assignment: DBQ Analysis**

5. DBQ Africa 2

    a. Target: I can create corroborative evidence to create an argument for a DBQ

    b. SFI: Missionaries, poverty, natives, colonial government

    c. **Assignment: DBQ Analysis**

6. Imperialism in Asia

    a. Target: I can compare imperialism in Asia with imperialism in Africa

    b. SFI: "Open," East Indies, dominion status, British Raj, sepoys, Empress of India, "traditional territorial aggrandizement," Siberia, Slavic, buffer state, Russo-Japanese War, "Open Door Policy," sphere of influence, Commodore Perry, Burma, Indochina, jingoism, Spanish–American War, pacify

    c. **Assignment: MI—Imperialism in Asia**

7. Responses to Imperialism

    a. Target: I can analyze the response by colonial powers in Africa and Asia to European conquest

    b. SFI: Traditionalists vs. modernizers, "new class," lowly jobs, sweatshops, segregation, master/slave relationship, Boxer Rebellion, Society of Harmonious Fists, spheres of influence, jingoism, shogun, samurai, Meiji Restoration, modernize, military state, Western imperialistic model, Western technology (examples), industrialization, Indian National Congress, global economy

    c. **Assignment: MI—Responses to Imperialism**

8. DBQ U.S. Imperialism

    a. Target: I can create corroborative evidence to create an argument for a DBQ

*(continued on next page)*

**Figure 9.1. Continued**

---

   b.  SFI: Orient, Monroe Doctrine, Roosevelt Corollary, Platt Amendment, "Open Door Policy," Anti-Imperialist League, Oceania, President William McKinley

   c.  **Assignment: DBQ Analysis**

9.  U.S. and the Philippines

   a.  Target: I can compare the role the United States played in the Philippines with the role Europe played in Africa and Asia

   b.  SFI: Filipino Insurrection, White Man's Burden, Black Man's Burden, atrocity, water cure (waterboarding)

   c.  **Assignment: Paideia Seminar Questions**

10. QFT Review and "Shooting an Elephant"

   a.  Target: I can evaluate the impact of imperialism on Europe, the United States, Asia, and Africa

   b.  SFI: Anglo-Burmese wars, Burma, India, British Empire, George Orwell

   c.  **Assignment: Paideia Seminar Questions; Compare and Contrast Imperialism**

11. Unit 4 Test

---

of the class and as a whole class for the second half. Inquiry takes time, but by flipping my classroom to focus on processing skills in class, we maximize efficiency together. Students are more likely to be willing to struggle if they see others struggling too. By flipping the classroom, my design ensures no student ever struggles alone to practice and we create an inclusive culture in the classroom. While I assign readings for this flip, which somewhat resembles traditional homework, teachers of students who struggle with reading might create videos of mini lectures acquainting students with the material or guidance to direct their reading. These videos might be posted on the school site, YouTube, or SchoolTube for students to access with phones, tablets, or computers.

Because I scaffold reading, writing, speaking, and argumentation tasks logically to help them respond to our sincere questions, my students are usually more ready to engage the inquiry cycle in more independent and authentic ways.

### Reading with Purpose

It's no surprise that it is difficult for students to analyze and synthesize historical texts, but corroborating sources, by comparing information and perspectives across disparate documents, and generalizing their themes and conflicting viewpoints, are nearly Herculean. Corroboration is an advanced skill, especially difficult and daunting for students, since it asks that they understand each document and then synthesize those documents and use them to produce a coherent and advanced argument. This difficulty makes it important to give my students plenty of practice reading historical documents in units prior to this one. In this unit alone, students read nearly 30 primary documents from the 1870s to the 1910s, but using DBQ developed by the DBQ Project, College Board, and other teachers as a resource, each text is small in size and scope and explicitly aligned with a DBQ. A third of the documents are images, and we work in collaborative groups to maximize our time developing skills for analysis, synthesis, and evaluation.

A major summative goal of this unit is to use documents to support argumentative writing by answering a DBQ, but a lot of prior preparation (scaffolding) goes into readying students for that daunting task. As a transitional unit, "Imperialism" introduces the DBQ format to students so they can practice interpreting documents corroboratively, categorizing them, and organizing thesis statements and topic sentences supported by SFI. Prior to this unit, we practice historical thinking skills, specifically, sourcing documents, identifying a document's point of view, and assessing contexts in which documents were created, followed by practice using these skills to develop generalizations corroborated with evidence to answer DBQs. Students are asked to describe:

- Source (who produced, when, where, why, to what audience and purpose?)
- Point of view (whose POV is included/excluded?)
- Contextualizing elements (events, people, themes of this era)
- Document analysis (main idea/ideas)

Figure 9.2 shows an analysis sheet for "Document C."

### Writing with Purpose

Writing—through main idea logs and generalization exercises—focuses on inductive and deductive reasoning and helps my students transition from single sentences to paragraph construction and eventually essay writing. In addition to developing their writing skills, I time my students and encourage them to think as they write. If the goal is to support students to compose a timed essay, then time management (a 21st-century thinking skill) must be addressed to teach decisionmaking under pressure. The flipped classroom approach enables students to focus on these skills with their peers and me as support during class time, which builds their efficacy and engagement.

I further use main idea logs to help students write and think about grade-level texts that usually are referred to in DBQs and to corroborate those texts in any response activities. In main idea logs, students read a primary or secondary document and write one clear, concise sentence that

**Figure 9.2. DBQ Analysis Sheet**

Sourcing (Who produce, when, why, where purpose/audience?):
Various to show purpose to world of technology
POV (Whose point of view included/excluded):
POV of europeans.
Contextualizing (Events, themes, people of this era):
Industrial rev. europeans
Document Analysis (MI):
Inventions made during the I.R. led to the need/abaility to colonize by making it easier to conquer lands.

**Document C: *Various***

| Technological Development (Date Invented) | Use and Significance |
| --- | --- |
| Steam engine first used in boats (1787); first used in locomotives (1804) | A more constant and forceful source of power than sails on ships or horse-drawn carriages<br><br>Steam engines powered ships and railroads |
| Method of getting quinine from cinchona tree bark (1820) | Treatment for the disease malaria |
| Electric telegraph (1837) | Communication over long distances |
| Bessemer process (1855) | Quicker and cheaper method of manufacturing steel, which was lighter and more durable than iron |
| Maxim gun (1884) | First machine gun |
| Repeating rifle (late 1800s) | A faster loading gun that was able to fire multiple shots more accurately than older muskets |

demonstrates the main idea of the document. Doing so helps my students demonstrate understanding of more difficult, above-grade-level texts too. This deductive exercise is instrumental in helping students focus on what to say while incorporating other sources into their work. When transitioning to the DBQ format, students use the main idea log to focus analysis on one source at a time. Doing this as they read lightens their cognitive load and enables them to practice corroborating multiple sources into defensible cate-

**Figure 9.3. Example of a Main Idea Log**

The Scramble for Africa

Europeans controlled relatively little of the African continent before 1880. Earlier, when their economic interests were more limited (in the case of Africa, primarily the slave trade), European states had generally been satisfied to deal with existing independent states rather than attempting to establish direct control over vast territories. For the most part, the Western presence in Africa had been limited to controlling the regional trade network and establishing a few footholds where the foreigners could carry on trade and missionary activity. During the last two decades of the nineteeth century, however the quest for colonies became a "**Scramble for Africa**" as all of the major European states engaged in a land grab.

Many Europeans decided they need resources from Africa.
All or countries!

gories. Figure 9.3 offers a good example, from one of my students, of break-ing down an excerpt from a college-level source into manageable chunks by identifying main ideas.

Generalization exercises, which I use a lot in formative assessments, require students to inductively group a series of several terms, in this case *jingoism, modernize, sweatshops, Boxer Rebellion, Meiji Restoration, seg-regation,* and *traditionalist* (as seen in Figure 9.4), based on what they have in common and then write a sentence that incorporates the terms into one clear, concise statement. This sentence becomes the topic sentence of their final essay, and the students choose one of the terms to write an interpretive commentary on wherein they construct a sentence that uses details about that term as evidence to support their topic sentence. Without realizing it, students are practicing inductive reasoning and paragraph construction in their writing, and learning to create body paragraphs that support their the-ses. I purposely use inductive reasoning because it helps my students create topic sentences for each body paragraph that back their theses and guide them to become independently able to generalize historical interpretations based on the specific factual information they study. The process provides students with confidence as they transition to writing on increasingly large scales until they are comfortable with essay writing. In the example of a generalization exercise task in Figure 9.4, note how the student discerns commonality between terms and self-assesses to refine her wording to reflect her responses. I encourage students to either use ink or avoid erasing to help them see their own thinking progress over time.

Once students are comfortable with generalization, I gradually have them use all of the terms in a practice timed-writing task that pressures them formatively to think about and write an in-class essay as quickly and clearly as they can, but only one paragraph at a time. If the end goal is for students to write a timed essay in class, they must practice writing against a clock. The first few times, I provide 12 minutes (more than they need) to ease them into the process. Once they see they can complete the exercise successfully, I start to limit their time by a minute each writing cycle until we work with 8 minutes total. Much to students' surprise, they are able to write as much

## Figure 9.4. Sample Generalization Exercise

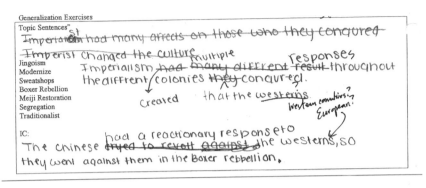

in 8 minutes as they did when they had in 12. Their self-efficacy skyrockets because of the design.

### DBQ Analysis—Combining Reading and Writing Within Inquiry

DBQs help students synthesize inquiry and assess reading and writing skills. Because this is a transitional unit, my goal is to expose students to DBQs to assess their readiness to start essay writing. Why DBQs? They are a clear, manageable way of connecting historical thinking and writing practices. The major task is to ensure students have enough practice opportunities with writing to be successful answering basic DBQs right away. I created a DBQ analysis sheet that enables students to focus on historical thinking elements (sourcing, point of view, and context) and apply those in writing (main idea logs, corroboration of texts, and thesis writing). Students get four topical, essential, *sincere* DBQs like:

1. Why did Europeans want Africa?
2. Who originally benefited from imperialism?
3. How has imperialism shaped U.S. policy?
4. Was/is imperialism moral?

The analysis sheet breaks down historical thinking into more manageable segments so students succeed more and earlier in making inferences and synthesizing generalities (see Figure 9.5).

The first times my students attempt corroborating evidence to establish a claim (write and support a thesis), the most difficult part for them usually is to distinguish elements in textual sources. For example, in Figure 9.5, the student's first and third categorizations overlap too much and need revision. But that's a good start for a novice historian!

Practicing responses to multiple DBQs doesn't always adequately prepare students for a culminating, individual summative writing response.

**Figure 9.5. Excerpt of a Document-Based Question Analysis Sheet**

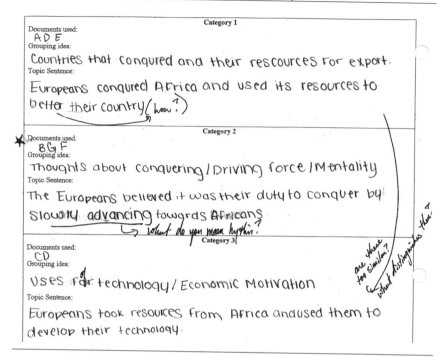

When needed, I change their assessment to a more traditional free-response style wherein they compare documents but don't have to make many formal citations to make an argument. A big take-away for this unit for me as a teacher is the need to more purposefully enable students to move from analyzing single sources to corroborating evidence earlier. When I teach it next time, I will create another step in the progression toward responses to DBQs. Earlier brief DBQ practice responses in other units will provide students more practice and confidence with historical thinking sooner, and their answers will be more sophisticated because of it.

## Communicating with Purpose—Deeper Meaning Through Student-Driven Questions

There are at least three student-centered tasks I intentionally bookend this unit with to enable deeper meaning based on what we discuss in class. The tasks include simulation, debate, and Paideia Seminars. Students need forums to express ideas in a safe community so they can practice developing arguments backed by evidence. While debates are one way of getting students to practice essay writing, I use two Paideia Seminars and a classroom simulation to foster student engagement with the intricacies of the imperialist mindset and its historical consequences.

The Paideia Seminar topics I used the last time I taught this unit were (1) U.S.–Filipino relations and (2) George Orwell's "Shooting an Elephant" (1981). For 2 days, students use Paideia Seminars to collaborate and explore how imperialism affected the mindsets of people who participated in and rejected it.

The U.S.–Filipino case study in imperialism sharpens students' skills in reading and prepares them for DBQ responses. It also focuses on what is often the part of this unit that students find most disturbing. Documents used include "The White Man's Burden," "The Black Man's Burden," anti-imperialist writings by Mark Twain, and contemporary scholarship examining U.S. use of segregated troops and war atrocities committed against Filipino insurgents—including examples of waterboarding that hold obvious and troubling modern relevance. Students produce questions for classmates based on key elements (e.g., White vs. Black, rich vs. poor, anti-imperialists vs. imperialist, and "benefits" of civilization).

The culminating seminar on Orwell's "Shooting an Elephant" reveals, for me, the soul of history, exposing in a raw way the feelings of those who suffer and succeed during major eras and the events that can overshadow individual lives. Literature, when used in social studies, helps students zero in on major themes. History blends information and interpretation; literature provides practice with identifying and discussing those interpretations and their themes. Orwell is masterful in representing imperial oppression and so subtly exposes its complexities that students are tricked into seeing its horrors from both sides. This epiphany doesn't always come from primary or secondary sources, so we embrace cross-disciplinary resources like literature to practice skills and enrich the context in which students respond to the sincere questions that frame their work together.

Once students engage the texts through inquiry, we explore applications to modern society. We look at international relations and popular culture for evidence of imperialism. Was the U.S. 2003 Iraqi invasion imperialistic? Examining the transition from the Bush doctrine to the Obama administration, is American culture hegemonic? Coca-Cola, Nike, and *The Avengers* are all American export products. Are they imperialistic too? The students inquire and respond. Other current examples may be found in TV shows like *The Walking Dead* and movies like *Star Wars* and *The Hunger Games*. The blend of historical and contemporary examples using multiple media and sincere document-based questions helps students see the enduring relevance that underlies imperialist history.

## CONCLUSION

The earliest known mention of the word *history* is traced to Herodotus. The Greek word means inquiry, or to gain knowledge through investigation.

*Nowhere* does history mean "a boring list of facts" or any other pejorative definition that strips its juxtaposition to the present. Social studies inquiry is exciting: Students ask complex questions, investigate sources, formulate interpretations, and come to see knowledge and skills as useful tools. With purpose and responsive teaching, I work to foster a symbiotic relationship between teacher and student where learning is a shared responsibility. Sincere questions invite students to unlock new doors; historical and contemporary sources provide the keys; and like Socrates on steroids, a purposeful teacher can blow a student's mind with intentionality.

This intentionality, this design, lends teachers and students their greatest potentials for success. In this unit I use teacher-guided inquiry to help students acquire skills needed to think and communicate historically. Because I engage them with documents, have them ask questions and respond, and enable them to practice in an intellectually safe environment, they are able to explore new topics, arrive at informed conclusions, and put themselves in positions to express those conclusions in writing and speaking. Skills, by nature, must be scaffolded to ensure the greatest success, and teachers must take care that the numerous working parts don't overload students' cognitive capacities. This unit is not the first or last time I teach these skills, but it is the first time students focus these skills for the purpose of drawing and communicating conclusions. Using evidence derived from inquiry and response, utilizing multiple media to engage students' understanding, refines both their knowledge and skills, and my own professional ability to shape instruction on purpose.

# CHAPTER 10

# Using Multiple Media on Purpose

In the pursuit of greater equality in our education system, from K to PhD, technology access, print literacies, and verbal skill all collide as requirements for even basic participation in an information-based, technology-dependent economy and society.

—Adam J. Banks

Various forms of media have been a boon and bane throughout history. Socrates railed against the newfangled practices of reading and writing, and convinced people that recording information instead of memorizing it would weaken their minds. Yes, reading and writing were once new technologies people found *dangerous*. Today such claims seem laughable, as reading and writing are esteemed as life skills. There has been a long tradition of criticizing new technology as corruption, from lamenting how television makes people dumb, pop music destroys morality, video games cause violence, or Twitter limits actual thought to 140-character snippets.

Although many criticize modern media, others see hope. Howe and Strauss (2009) think the array of media and technology today creates an incredible level of awareness and a strong sense of problem solving, so that Millennials may just be "the next great generation." Teens today have unprecedented access to information via multiple media. Aside from the near-universal ownership of televisions, "93% of US teens have a computer or access to one" (Madden, Lenhart, Duggan, Cortesi, & Gasser, 2013, p. 5), and "78% of teens now have a cell phone, and almost half (47%) of those own smartphones. That translates into 37% of all teens who have smartphones, up from just 23% in 2011" (p. 2). Additionally, "about three in four (74%) teens ages 12–17 say they access the Internet on cell phones, tablets, and other mobile devices at least occasionally" (p. 2). More than ever before, access means students can make media, consume it, interact with people across the world, and also learn in ways formerly impossible.

Good or bad, media ubiquity cannot be ignored. It's part of students' realities. To ignore that is to risk making school obsolete and irrelevant. In this chapter we espouse ways to engage students in learning that integrate media and scholastic experiences. Print is no longer the only or even primary source of information and entertainment for 21st-century youth, as people now interact daily with texts conveyed by televisions, computers, video games, phone apps, and other technologies. These new media texts are so abundant they "no longer just shape our culture—they are our culture" (Thoman & Jolls, 2004, p. 18). Instead of putting our heads in the sand, we strive to purposely use these tools to help students think critically about their media, be responsible users of technology, and understand and explore the world in deeper ways.

In order to create relevant curriculum, supportive environments, and responsive teaching (Chapter 2), and encourage motivation and engagement (Chapter 3), we need to capitalize on students' funds of knowledge (Chapter 4). Using the multiple media they're immersed in, we can create classrooms where everyone can be a primary knower with something to offer (Aukerman, 2007). But although we think it is essential to acknowledge and include all types of texts, teachers also must ensure those multiple media are always used thoughtfully with clear purpose.

## CRITICAL CONVERSATIONS ABOUT MEDIA

In addition to portraying the world to today's learners in different terms compared with traditional academic texts, multiple new media offer us the opportunity to question the conventions these new media follow. The most commonly asked questions in critical media literacy tasks offer a sturdy framework for reading comprehension in any subject area. For instance, the Center for Media Literacy (2003) provides five questions for critical media study:

1. Who created the message?
2. What creative techniques are used to attract my attention?
3. How might different people understand this message differently from me?
4. What lifestyles, values, and points of view are represented in—or omitted from—this message?
5. Why is this message being sent?

These questions examine concrete and abstract ideas while providing a platform for critical thinking and discussion. We've used these questions with many students, from middle schoolers to teacher education candidates, to analyze media and examine how they portray similar things in variable useful ways. We've found them quite useful and highly applicable in all content areas. We will explore just how we have applied these questions in those content areas in the sections below.

## WHEN MEDIA LITERACY IS CRITICAL

Two seeming drawbacks of incorporating critical media literacy in classrooms are the inability to fully control discussion, and to always teach a specific curriculum topic via traditional methods. Some teachers feel that taking time to hear students share their views and opinions is mostly useless, or that such talk is inefficient and takes time better spent covering standards. Others might not like the loss of control that accompanies such critical media class discussions (Fecho & Botzakis, 2007).

However, critical media literacy has significant rewards. First, critical discussions about content and texts encourages students to participate (Johnson & Freedman, 2005). To create a learning environment where all students can join in actively, critical media literacy tasks tap into an area where many students, especially those who feel marginal, are experts. Think about it. Students have little to say regarding when they come to school, their schedules, what they have to do in class, when they eat, or even when they go to the bathroom. They have long been subjected to the rules, whether those rules were justified or not. By the time they reach middle school, they have long contended with schoolwork and been required to read academic texts. They know what it's like to feel powerless, and they have serious thoughts and knowledge about it. Their insights can drive critical responses to texts and tasks, helping peers relate to the issues and content they study.

Second, exploring critical media literacy brings into classrooms texts that students use in daily life. Many things students do every day involve reading nonprint and media texts, so there is a reduced cognitive load for them as readers. With less need to learn background or contextual knowledge (because the students already come to school with significant knowledge of language, or a literary theme, or a scientific practice or topic, or a historical event/issue), students can focus more on immediate comprehension. Perhaps most positive, being such experts lends high self-efficacy and promotes positive engagement that may be a welcome and new experience for some (Alvermann, 2001; O'Brien, 2001).

When learners can use what they already know in their lives in new ways, they can demonstrate expertise that transforms what and how teachers teach. Students who engage in critical media literacy are more likely to draw on their prior knowledge to comprehend new ideas (Hobbs, 2007). Instead of focusing simply on details such as memorizing equations or identifying cause and effect, discussions across subject areas can gravitate toward more complex and richer problems, solutions, or other tasks for student response and learning. Students can critique a wider range of resources. Critical media literacy is an excellent entry point for students to find value for engaging in their own educations.

We want to be clear: Bringing media into any classroom is not about dumbing things down for millennial youth who "can't" or "won't" engage traditional resources. We use multiple media to frame learning situations wherein students can more successfully use prior knowledge to their advantage. The nonprint and multiple media they read every day can be used to teach many academic skills and learning strategies. Teachers can promote participation by allowing students to apply familiar text formats they feel comfortable with. Used in conjunction with traditional academic texts, multiple media support rather than hinder motivation, engagement, and achievement. In what follows, we address how to make such connections using media to teach skills necessary in different content areas.

## WHAT COUNTS AS READING?

Nowadays, education has been influenced by "cross-disciplinary fertilization" (Hobbs, 2007, p. 6) between literary, cultural, media, and communication studies, resulting in a broad and more encompassing concept of *text* and what it means to read. We use *texts* to mean "forms of symbolic expression that convey meaning from authors to readers" (Hobbs, 2007, p. 7). That includes words, but also images, sounds, colors, patterns, movements, and/or other things that can be interpreted (i.e., that can be *read*).

Throughout history, the concept of reading has been applied to a number of communication acts, including the abilities to identify emotion from facial expressions or body language, get subtext from "the writing on the wall," track animal movements from their footprints, predict future events from tea leaves, and determine geological eras of the past from rock strata in valleys (Manguel, 1997). Just in these examples, this definition of reading enables inclusion in language arts, mathematics, physical sciences, and social sciences. Today, people read in a variety of ways, including online contexts, television viewing, and interactive video games that use combinations of text, image, sound, and movement. However, a notion persists in schools that print texts are the only important ones to study, even when many students struggle to understand them in isolation.

When reading in school, comprehension is important but often taken for granted as the first task on the way to more in-depth analyses. Marginalized readers may find it difficult to do such analyses, as they may be more familiar with traditional school activities allegedly designed to raise their test scores by skill and drill (Meier & Wood, 2004). More abstract tasks demanded of them in middle school may not be so familiar, but critical media tasks help students make more meaningful connections with content and see the ultimate goals of learning. Students' familiarity with different media is a powerful but often neglected resource. It is a boon to analyzing texts, as studying topics across multiple media alleviates a number of comprehension issues that can accompany reading print texts alone.

In this chapter, we look at texts without limiting ourselves to printed words. We look to television commercials, apps, movies, songs, games, websites, and almost any other item we can "read." To develop greater understandings of these media and show how they can help in school, we first look at how they are structured. Then we present tasks that cross over a number of not only media but also content areas, from language arts to social studies to science to math and beyond.

## A KINDER, GENTLER KIND OF GRAMMAR

If you're like us, most of your memories of grammar study are pretty bleak. Diagramming sentences, remembering not to split infinitives (or was it to not split them?), or stressing over sentence fragments—such traditions have scarred many a learner. But here we talk about grammar in the sense of how texts are structured. All texts have a logic, or set of rules that makes them work. English teachers are probably familiar with literary grammars, which include familiar concerns like conventional spelling, sentence construction, semantics, tone, plot structure, and symbolism, among other things. But other technologies also use grammars to convey meaning (New London Group, 1996), even though those grammars may seem different, impossibly complex, utterly obvious, or even invisible. Just as it's a central goal in English to grammatically analyze print, it is also important to examine, break down, and teach the grammars used to build other texts we use as resources and tools. It can be difficult to identify what features to focus on, teach, and use in class. Below, we include examples of multiple media grammars that can be used more purposefully across content areas to promote learning.

### Books

Books are certainly one of the oldest types of media. They probably are also most familiar to educators, so we won't go into much detail about how their elements work. In terms of literature, plot and character are what many attend to while reading, but analyses of narrative structure, figurative language, conflicts, symbolism, and themes are also parts of reading.

That said, some books are nonfiction or textbooks and don't really use narrative conventions. They explain concepts, describe historical events or figures, detail instructions for science experiments, or describe ways to solve numeric problems. What really helps steer readers to success is explicit teaching of text structures and text features. *Structures* are ways that text is logically organized, including lists, sequences, main ideas, or causes and effects. *Features* are conventions that indicate specific meanings; for instance, bold text indicates significance while italics can indicate a title, a foreign word, or emphasis. Some features figure into how text structures work. For instance, if you see bullet points while reading, you're probably dealing with a list structure. Learning that increases the ability to understand meaning.

## Film/Television

In speaking about visual media such as film or television, teachers and students should become familiar with the terms associated with those media, just as they are with print texts. Doing so builds a vocabulary and framework readers can use just as when they learn vocabulary associated with studying traditional elements of literature (Kist, 2005). Helping students read visual media requires specific knowledge of how nonlinguistic communication works in film and TV, including long shots or close-ups, camera pans, scene transitions, jump-cut edits, camera angles, pacing, and framing. Additionally, directorial choices like lighting, blocking, music, and costuming also generate systematic meanings.

These visual characteristics help indicate genre. For instance, if we know we are watching a romantic comedy, we expect a couple will fall in love, face crises, and then reunite for a happy ending. Over the course of the story, we expect to find lots of visual shorthand, such as a close-up shot of lovers locking eyes or kissing to communicate their affection, or a shot of someone slamming a door and walking away as a point of conflict. When the couple is in crisis, slow, sad music might play on the soundtrack. If there is a wedding at the end, there is a montage of characters' faces to show their emotions and resolve their stories, or perhaps there is a larger group shot to suggest the idea of a new family—a union, which is the definition of traditional comedy.

All of these features are grammatical, strategically planned by filmmakers to help readers make sense of the text just as words are manipulated by authors to create meaningful books. With this analogy, studying film grammars can make for great comparisons with devices and techniques that many concrete learners struggle with in literary and informational reading. Films and documentaries also use symbolism, for example, but in ways most readers are almost automatically familiar with, far more so than in their reading of print-based texts. We don't have space to delineate all the grammatical features of film or their analogs in print-based texts here, but a good reference for teachers about using film and television is Golden's *Reading in the Dark* (2001).

## Graphic Novels

As with film, graphic novels have their own grammar, a complex symbol system that teachers can use to explain literacy concepts and academic concepts. The grammar of graphic novels is based on panels, gutters, angles, facial expressions, motion lines, and word balloons, features that make specific meaning (Jacobs, 2007; McCloud, 1993). Panels are the squares that contain images of action; gutters are the space between panels where time is assumed to elapse; motion lines usually depict someone running or falling down; and word balloons contain information or character speech.

Graphic novels also feature what Yang (2008) calls visual permanence, the idea that an image creates an illusion of motion and time passing while remaining static. Visual permanence can be a useful way for students to understand figurative language in academic print-based texts, deepen print-based meaning, and make it more accessible. For example, it can be used to demonstrate how images in a suspenseful text (fiction or nonfiction) create tone by indicating that a setting is sinister or scary based on a series of dark and increasingly smaller panels. Comparing such a technique in graphic novel grammar with a more literary one like in a text by Edgar Allan Poe helps students learn multiple ways of producing effects using both print and nonprint. In such a way, graphic visual grammars help readers understand how figurative or symbolic language works.

### Video Games

Once available only in arcades, video games are now in our homes as part of game consoles and apps on our phones. They've long been denounced for their content, either too violent or too vapid. They've also been easy for some to blame for dumbing children down or creating a population of passive citizens. More recently, however, they have been amassing more academic advocates who have identified ways they contain and exercise various fundamental learning principles (Gee, 2003). These include understanding symbols, promoting identity, fostering problem solving and persistence, basic reading practice, and evaluating design principles. At least one study showed that playing video games helped struggling readers, specifically dyslexic youth, in terms of reading fluency as well as sustained attention (Franceschini et al., 2013). Other researchers (e.g., Steinkuehler, 2010) have promoted video games because they offer a space for many to demonstrate expertise, experience success, and realize their capabilities in low-risk environments during practice.

## THE AFFORDANCES OF MEDIA

Media as described here cover a wide range, from print to electronic to audio. Many features can be included in such multiple grammars and vary widely. Mainly, what we can say about all media formats is they are meant to grab and hold attention (Lanham, 2001). Specific features are manipulated to structure media and attract attention to convey specific messages, and that is the focus of critical media instruction across all subjects.

In the case of print advertisements, fonts, font size, color, and layout influence how meaning is conveyed. Consider how a newspaper's front page draws readers' eyes to particular graphics or headlines on purpose. In television commercials, strong images, soundtracks, quick cuts, and movement are central features that structure meaning. They usually include memorable music and colors to elicit comfort, desire, and pleasure in viewers.

There is not space enough here to describe all media grammars, and our examples are illustrative but not at all exhaustive. Varied media in content-area teaching have great potential to support student engagement, and the raw materials they offer for thought, appreciation, and analyses are not only available but rich and plentiful. What's more, multiple media are part and parcel of students' lived worlds every day. They not only need familiarity with these genres and conventions to learn better in school. They also need to be well-practiced in interpreting them and using them in relevant ways. In what follows we describe tasks that draw on these texts and their grammars for purposeful teaching.

One aspect of critical thinking is to critique the world around us. But another aspect involves viewing the world through multiple lenses to gain new perspectives on ideas and fresh insights for solving problems. Considering critical thinking and how it can be engaged via multiple media, we think of the term *affordances* (Gaver, 1991)—the resources gained from an object through its use. The properties of the object and its relationship to the person using it make certain actions possible. In the case of digital media like video games and phone apps, users are afforded multiple opportunities to explore identities, roles, and worlds across subjects in interesting ways.

### Science: Thinking Like a Virus

Pandemic 2 (www.crazymonkeygames.com/Pandemic-2.html) is a game where the player is the ultimate villain: A virus that is spreading worldwide. The game's objective is to infect as many people as possible, and play requires strategy. Not only must players know routine types of contagion, but they must learn geography, sociology, and political science in order to optimally navigate the game. Outcomes speak to biology, medicine, and many aspects of the social sciences such as psychology and history. What too often has been lazily dismissed as low-culture tomfoolery (digital games) is actually an excellent simulation of how diseases spread and how humans respond. By assuming the role of the enemy in such games, students learn how to protect themselves, consider how systems work, make predictions, experiment with strategies, and perhaps become proactive and ambitious to support the public health of others in the future.

### Math: What? You Don't Remember How to Do Algebra?

Many students fear mathematics. We bet many reading this book are rowing in that same boat. But there are a great number of interactive websites and programs on the Internet available to help. One of the most helpful is Al-

gebra Touch (www.regularberry.com/), an app for iPhones or iPads where
users solve equations or simplify expressions with the touch of a finger. We
know counting on fingers is pretty much unacceptable after kindergarten,
but this app helps users add, multiply, subtract, and divide in ways where
the numbers and variables move. Because they are on a screen and not a
printed page, it's easier to see how they relate to one another and interact.
Like terms literally move graphically to one side of the app's interface and
cancel each other out to show users how the math works. That clear visual
is a powerful way to help confused students see what's actually going on
with all those equations. The app provides users an alternative modality
to *see* problem solving. It offers a window into the basics of what is one
of the most commonly taught but (for many) intimidating school subjects
there is.

### Social Studies: Politics and Propaganda via Presidential Election Commercials

The Living Room Candidate (www.livingroomcandidate.org/) is a website
devoted to chronicling television commercials used in U.S. presidential elec-
tions. They are all on the page, from 1952 until now, presenting a video
series that shows the political machinations, historical movements, personalities, and events of the past century. These videos are about how history
is made and shaped, and also how narratives we use today were made and
perpetuated.

It is a fascinating site that allows students to perform multiple tasks.
They can examine how commercial design has changed over time, with the
relatively staid images of yesteryear contrasting startlingly with the more
frenetic representations of today. They can see how specific rhetorics of
hope, fear, and patriotism have played out over time. They can see how
political messages have transformed from the blatant (such as Lyndon Johnson's "Daisy Girl" ad depicting the nuclear destruction that would result
from his opponent's election) to the relatively more subtle ways contemporary politicians advance their agendas via images and sound bites. Students
can see which tactics have been employed time and again, and which have
been rarely used.

There are opportunities to do comparisons over time, between com-
peting candidates, or even of political parties' similarities and differences.
Students can see how people have been framed and characterized by mass
media ads, for good or ill. They can identify ways in which political ads
attempt to manipulate viewer emotional reactions and judgments. They can
view progressions of ads from a candidate over time to see what her message was and how it developed. Put simply, there is much here to study,
in terms of both the media itself and also historical significance, how this
genre of political ads begins as a relatively fluid concept and solidifies over

time. It would be difficult to think about and discuss such ideas using print texts alone. TV commercials provide an amplified text set and additional platform.

## Language Arts: Exploring Characterization Using Reality Television

Just as the authors of novels use certain details or descriptions about characters so readers draw certain conclusions, so do directors and stars of reality television programs. Even though such shows ostensibly are not scripted (and allowing that some might not be appropriate for teaching in school), they are presented in ways that convey narrative progressions. Taking our cue from Howley (2007), English teachers can use clips from reality shows to explore character development, one of the most frequently studied literary elements.

On *The Voice*, for instance, viewers come to know various contestants in a chronological sequence. First, we see many hopefuls audition. Over time, the producers whittle down the contestant pool. Then they present more about individual stars' backgrounds, introduce their particular styles and tastes, and establish their personalities for the purposes of the program. Some become villains, others champions, and some even jokes. In their competition, viewers see contestants adapt to shifting circumstances, including song genres, performance types, and pressure scenarios. Viewers follow this narrative specifically to enjoy and consider each contestant's growth and abilities, from baby-faced beginners to polished performers.

Working with *The Voice* as a text, teachers can show students clips of one of the singers and then have learners write about what each performance says about the artist as the narratives progress. Students can discuss opinions and provide evidence to support arguments. Technical aspects— lighting choices, camera angles, special effects, and choreography—become focal points for analyses of the program's grammar. Students also can evaluate contestants' choices: songs, costumes, use of instruments, and the personae they adopt for performances.

In this task, character study is done in a medium in which many students are fully knowledgeable and comfortable. They watch such programs every day outside school. Taking the opportunity to study how producers' choices in making TV shows as they do shape viewers' thoughts and perceptions and can help students become more aware of how they interact with and use media. Over several episodes, they can explore how such shows use narrative and images to attract viewers and sell ideas or products. In the end, development of a unique personality is just as important as talent in such a competition, and in effect the singers are all creating characters to promote themselves as much as possible. We can study that with students to learn academic content with relevant purposes.

## CONCLUSION

Media can be seen as a spoonful of sugar that helps the learning go down, or as a way of catching students' attention by entertainment. But we hope we have shown that multiple media in classroom instruction afford us all much more for education success. Media are integral to students' lives. This doesn't mean today's youth are crippled or stunted by media's presence. It does mean their lives and worlds are fully integrated with media to the point that not using them to teach in school is nearly unethical if we seek to be responsive teachers for student success. It is difficult to remember what life was like before cellphones, GPS, DVRs, or computers, mostly because they're now realities we take for granted. They're not going away, and to ignore them in classrooms is to ignore a large part of our own and our students' worlds. By neglecting to incorporate multiple media in our subject-area instruction, we risk showing students that what they learn in school is divorced from reality, useless, and largely irrelevant to their futures. Students need to see what happens in school as relating to their lives and their worlds, and as of right now that means having to truck with technology and media. This does *not* mean we have to discard our beloved books, paper, and pens. It *does* mean we have to work harder to bridge older technologies with those of today. We must show that what we teach in school is not obsolete, but exists in conjunction with the tools people make and use to act in life. In Chapter 11, we demonstrate how media can be used as we describe using a unit plan from English language arts.

# Model Unit Plan 4
## An Odyssey into Multiple Media

*Katie Raby,*
*Grace Christian Academy, Knoxville, TN*

In some of my classes, my greatest challenge as an English teacher is getting students to actually read print-based, canonical, and traditional literature. I teach high school students who aren't necessarily going to college and have had multiple negative experiences with books. They feel they already know the outcomes of their trying. They're frequently resigned to the fact they are poor readers who cannot grasp figurative language, cannot do literary analysis right, do not find joy in reading, or simply cannot comprehend what they read. So what I find I have to do early on is use tactics that show them what they *are* capable of and good at, to build their efficacy and confidence, particularly at the start of the year with the unit I present here. It strategically integrates traditional literature with multiple types of other media my students recognize and use every day. I find this unit energizes most if not all my students, and it helps set up future opportunities for them to find success not just in this unit but over the course of the entire school year.

### ACTIVATING STUDENT PRIOR KNOWLEDGE

One of the main functions of English language arts (ELA) classes is to prepare students to use language in exact ways, be precise with their terms, and communicate clearly in different contexts for varied purposes and audiences. Many times, approaching those goals involves using technical vocabulary and jargon that feels arcane. Basic concepts like thesis statements, figurative language, and symbolism can become barriers to literal-minded or already bewildered students. In order to not ignore but respond to their status as novices, I begin by introducing literary ideas in direct and concrete ways. For instance, I combine aspects of literary analysis with those of media literacy. My students might not be strong readers of *print*, but they all know how to navigate the Internet, use cellphones, play video games, and participate in social media networks. Having assessed that these are elements of my students' funds of knowledge, I try to build from those to make a bridge from their lived experiences to what we will do with academic content in ELA class.

## FOCUSED LEARNING TARGETS TO INCREASE SUCCESS

I begin by focusing on one of the most dreaded areas of ELA, grammar. This topic may provoke traumatic flashbacks in some readers, but I don't mean grammar in the stilted, let's-all-diagram-sentences sense. In this unit we apply grammar concepts later on and more in the sense of design, as in how media texts are composed and arranged on purpose by authors (including my students). The main task from the onset is to read a graphic novel adaptation of a classic piece of literature, but because many students are more familiar with talking about grammar via analysis of print text than via sequential nonprint texts like graphic novels in a school setting, I kick off the opening lesson with an extremely short story, just six words long. Mary Gaitskill's "Father died. Mother triumphed. I left" (The Hemingway Challenge, 2005, p. 92) is a simply told tale that allows for a lot of discussion as to its meaning. Plus, it is so short as to not be scary and literary for them to read ("It's a trap!"). Because I design it this way, students may not realize they are analyzing text fluently until after they've already finished and succeeded. Then I can praise them and help them go deeper with confidence.

After getting a minute or two to write down what they think the story means, my students share their thoughts, which range widely. Some turn the story into a murder tale where the mother has killed her husband either because he was abusive or because she wanted his money, with the fed-up child leaving or escaping at the end. Some interpret the story as the father dying from a disease, the mother getting over the loss, and the implied child ("I") growing up and leaving home. Still others look at it as a story about a sickly, beloved man whose death left a child in the care of a mean mother, with the child leaving home as soon as she was old enough. Students usually refer to the "I" as a female because that's the author's gender. In the ensuing discussions, we hypothesize about who the narrator is, what the order of the sentences adds to the story, and how as readers we know we are right or legitimate in our interpretations. In the end, students systematically are guided to see how much their own backgrounds contribute to the meanings they make when they read, but they also see how writers' choices influence their interpretations of texts. By the end of the task, we have practiced many of the skills required for analysis in English class and succeeded in full.

After discussing the mechanics and meaning of that tiny short story, the students turn their attention to a similar discussion using a comic strip. I use Charles Schultz's *Peanuts* episode from November 11, 2009, which is a short scene between Linus and his sister Lucy. Linus shows her his report card, beaming about receiving an A, only to learn that the A was the principal's middle initial. This tale is economically told in four panels of combined images and text. Together my students and I break down how we understand the story those panels tell. Students explain why they know Linus is running at one point (because of the position of his feet, the shadow shown below him, and the lines behind him symbolizing motion), how they know he is happy (because he is drawn with his smile as a large semicircle that takes up half his face), and how far away he is from Lucy (about 20 feet, because she is large in the foreground and he is small in the background). All this information is expressed in the first panel alone, and because the students are typically comfortable with understanding visual images, they can successfully do a close read of the strip and explain what they understand and assume automatically. If I used only print, I wouldn't be able to give them these crucial first opportunities to learn, practice, and succeed toward engagement with more difficult or less familiar readings.

This talk gets at the point that authors and artists make intentional choices to convey meaning, and also that, as readers, people use certain conventions to make meaning. This common work of literary analysis applies as much to reading a comic strip as it does to reading short stories or other print texts like poems and novels. At this point I extend our conversation from looking at how we make inferences when reading to naming the conventions that allow us to make meaning, so that students have the vocabulary needed to express themselves intelligently as primary knowers during classroom tasks. As a group, we brainstorm a list of technical words for analyzing sequential art. This list contains the following terms: panels, gutters, negative space, word balloons, thought balloons, color, shading, motion lines, pacing, and symbolic conventions (things like stars, hearts, light bulbs, or other shorthand). I make sure students copy down this list because they will immediately use it in our next task: beginning to read a graphic novel as a whole class.

A graphic novel is a hybrid text that is structured using styles and techniques my students are already comfortable with and ideas about textuality that I want them to engage with and that are new or less familiar to them as novices. Over time, I have found that in any given class about half of my students are familiar with reading graphic novels while half are not. So I begin at the beginning, talking about graphic novels, first defining what they are. In order to engage students from the very beginning of this lesson, I solicit their responses very enthusiastically, usually receiving a smattering of tentative responses about how graphic novels are kind of like comic books, are often about superheroes, or are like *anime* (Japanese cartoons). Once we have some ideas about what kind of text we are working with, we proceed to our next task of figuring out how to read and make sense of that kind of text in relation to others.

## GENERATING RELEVANT LEARNING TASKS

Gareth Hinds's version of Homer's *Odyssey* (2010) is a beautifully rendered and researched book that hews closely to the original canonical text. I assign students to pair up and read the first five pages using sticky notes to show where they see various sequential art conventions used by the author to create meanings or effects. Then I ask them to report to the whole group what they have found. Going page by page, I invite students to take part in close reading and report what they notice. They speak about the author's use of pacing and negative space as they notice the story begins with a wide landscape shot and then narrows in on particular locales. They speak of how the coloring in each illustration differentiates characters who are gods from those who are mere humans, and how that coloring also shows when a god appears in a mortal disguise. They also speak about how the author indicates people's relationships by positioning drawings of their figures in rooms and various other settings. Because Hinds uses his visuals very strategically and mindfully (and clearly), the students have much they can process and speak about. They learn to read graphic novels using the same technical expertise expected for other literary readings. Thus, I scaffold students' understanding of graphic novels toward literary *print* reading for academic learning, and also further apprentice them into the work of literary analysis and communication for life.

This focus on graphic novels creates a context for everything I wish to accomplish in my class. Following these introductory exercises, students undertake many tasks, including participating in classroom discussions, think-pair-share sessions, individual analyses, and essay writing. I have found graphic novels are of great assistance especially in that last endeavor of essay writing, because students can easily find references whenever they need evidence to support a claim they might make, compared with searching through a denser print-based novel for the details they need. The visual aspects of the text make more of an impression and are more readily used in synthesizing information without dumbing down any ELA content. The essays that result are usually some of the best of the year, because they are full of rich supporting evidence and better developed ideas resulting from my integration of the students' funds of knowledge and a type of media they normally aren't allowed to use seriously during school. Using this sort of formative task set at the beginning of the term is most useful, as the sort of composition we use as a summative assignment models everything my students will need for use and success in other assignments down the road.

In addition to all the text work and close reading we do together, students also have opportunities to compare versions of the same story across multiple media. They read and explicate particular passages from the graphic adaptation, such as the scene with the Cyclops, for instance. I also provide print-based text from the original epic poem so that they can identify and evaluate how Hinds adapted the original to make a new, fresh version. We compare what is contained and communicated within each version. In addition, we selectively view a different version of the same tale from the television mini-series starring Armand Assante (available on DVD) to get yet another take on the matter from digital video media. Watching the video is not just a time to take a break and be rewarded, as often is communicated when teachers break out the A/V equipment. In my class it is a time to study the techniques and choices that directors and actors use to make their own new adaptations of a story or text. Not only do we get at the technical aspects of film and other media as a result and talk about those media grammars, but we also gain the outcomes from translating a single work across multiple modes using different ways of composing texts that matter for today and the future. I have students talk about how mood is created in each mode, how characters are portrayed, and how the plot progresses differently in each (and why). Students talk about what was effective in each version, and which version (if any) might be the optimal way of telling that particular story. We also get into contrasting opinions here, using evidence from our readings to explore how authors might have made different choices adapting the work the students have just read and experienced. Students enjoy playing the role of critic, especially when I position them as primary knowers and experts, and they typically *are* experts when talking about pictures from a graphic novel or images in a video. But I do not let them just settle for critiquing the work of others. I also design tasks requiring students to participate in the creative composition process themselves.

The summative task for this unit is to create a graphic adaptation of some sort, either in sequential art or video form, always set in a different time period than the original text of *The Odyssey*. Some choose to act out their scripted adaptations as plays, another media mode, but these can easily be combined with the paper/art presentation if students prefer to demonstrate their understandings and learning more precisely in that particular format. Students' adaptations demonstrate that they comprehend major textual concepts from our readings, that they can use artful and mindful techniques to convey meaning and understand how others use them too, and that they have learned to transfer a scene from any given text to multiple other modes and contexts. Often, this final project results in students developing some humorous elements too, which shows me they are not only learning basic knowledge but making fluent personal connections while demonstrating comprehension. I purposely use this same type of task later in the year with *Romeo and Juliet*, or whichever Shakespearean play we read, to help them sustain and extend their reading knowledge and abilities, and this unit is the model that sets us all off on the right foot.

## CONCLUSION

I must tell you all as readers that the culminating activity for this unit is often one of the happiest times of the school year for me and my students. We all are extremely entertained by the multiple performance pieces we create, whether they are live dramatic re-enactments, YouTube videos, or gigantic comic strips. It also does me good as a professional to notice the ways different and new students use media each time, as media types and textuality evolve, to create and communicate their understandings of the various things we read. It tells me something when my students choose Barack and Michelle Obama as stand-ins for Odysseus and Penelope—not that they are merely picking convenient figures, but that they are internalizing understandings about the stature of mythic figures in classic literary texts and casting them in a more modern light via new and multiple media. At first it might seem silly to see Odysseus's challenge for his wife's would-be suitors, an elaborate display of strength involving a bow, arrow, and multiple axe heads, translated into a few teenagers throwing tennis balls at one another and deem that a legitimate academic task for learning language arts. But it actually shows great student ingenuity and also fluent abilities to use knowledge and experience from their lived worlds to learn new academic content in school. They were problem solving all the way, and while their choices might not be the most obvious or the ones we as experts might choose ourselves, they show me my students are thinking, analyzing, connecting, making meaning, and learning to communicate their understandings to an audience. These are all primary outcomes of studying English and meeting its traditional standards.

When I ask students at the end of the school year, they always say that the instructional unit I describe here was their favorite. They say it made English and reading feel easy to them. I can tell you that we put in a lot of time reading, talking, and thinking about all the texts each time. And the planning and composing of their presentations take time too, but with our explicit goals and clearly useful purposes, my students do not feel that work is onerous, not even a little. They *enjoy* and appreciate the opportunities to express themselves in different media, certainly, but the entire enterprise relies on their familiarity and expertise with those media, and that is why as a purposeful teacher I use them. Reading graphic novels and making multiple media adaptations may seem daunting at first, but my students do it and find it highly supportive in their learning about literary interpretation, reading, writing, thinking, and communicating their own ideas, all of which can be challenging if those same students are provided with only traditional print-based academic texts and tasks. The combination of media they read is our gateway to the learning we do in English class. It works because it includes my students' knowledge, interests, and experiences, and because it purposely and responsively helps them realize they are more familiar with what I'm teaching them than they might have thought at first. It helps them realize they can meet my challenges and grow. Using media, my students and I learn more on purpose.

# CHAPTER 12

# Conclusion

## Teaching on Purpose

> Productivity is never an accident. It is always the result of commitment to excellence, intelligent planning, and focused effort.
>
> —Paul J. Meyer

Thus far, we have written about what responsive teaching is and how to engage your students using their funds of knowledge as a resource. We also have laid out how to plan instruction by using purposeful designs, asking sincere questions, and incorporating multiple types of media. As we said in our introduction and as many readers already know: "Teaching is really, really, *really* hard work." This point bears repeating.

No matter how prepared one thinks one is or how many years of experience one amasses, there will still be times and places where things do not go as planned. There will be times that you will face adversity and something will not go your way. What seems like a great idea Sunday night can turn out to crash and burn on Monday morning. What works for first and second period may be a dud come third period, for no discernible reason. These things are to be expected: We all work with people. And people frequently can be unpredictable.

That last point often is lost in discussions about education. Some folks speak as if there are magic bullets, quick fixes, or tricks that work every time and in every context. They go on as if no one has ever thought to tackle the problems in education, and that they have the one solution. If there were such a product or practice that worked universally for educating people, we would be using it right now and would have from the get-go. Instead, we have to use our smarts, wits, and expertise to approach our diverse student populations, content areas, and classrooms successfully. And as we said and many readers know from their own classrooms, results sometimes will vary.

At the current time, it may seem like the entire teaching profession has been given a body blow. Teachers have been blamed for everything from poor test scores to declining moral standards. For-profit organizations and entrepreneurs gain more ground in privatizing education. Boxed and scripted instructional programs purport to make teaching "dummy-proof," as if following a script or lock-step set of procedures can respond to every student's needs. The number of people entering teacher preparation programs is falling. Levels of teacher burnout are rising, and more and more often people are leaving the profession by their 5th year. Also, a good number of the groups who claim to be interested in helping ailing schools treat the profession like teaching is a 2-year social work opportunity that anyone can do with minimal training.

This last point sticks in our craw because it neglects the intellectual and professional aspects of teaching. The notion that teachers are glorified saviors or miracle workers is deeply ingrained in our culture. As Carter (2009) has noted, this view is reflected in a myriad of feel-good movies where teachers defy the odds, buck the system, and deliver hope and success in the face of failure and despair. These stories are uplifting, and they make us feel good. They inspire people, but they also are somewhat disingenuous. They never show teachers planning or grading. They do not show all the preparation and planning that go into being an effective instructor. They make it seem that all a person has to do to create positive learning is to be able to spout some fiery rhetoric, stand up on a desk, or have students physically rip out the preface of their textbooks. You know that is just not the case. But more important, these persistent notions detract from what makes teachers successful, namely, some sense of competency, continuity, and consistency.

## THOSE THREE Cs

The ideas of competency, continuity, and consistency sum up what we have been discussing about the enterprise of teaching. Competency entails being professionally prepared, that is, going through a rigorous and substantial training program. It is not enough to want to work with children; we also have to do right by them. That means being highly knowledgeable not only of content but of various pedagogical methods that we might need to rely on for instruction. Teaching transcends just liking to work with children, being charitable with one's time, or going into a high-needs area as if you were in the Peace Corps. Teaching is an intellectual pursuit, and it must be treated as such.

Continuity means being part of a system that supports students and teachers, creating a positive, productive atmosphere for learning. Although it may seem that one teacher makes a difference in a student's life, that difference cannot be made unless an environment exists where teaching and learning are fostered by many, not just those in the classroom or school. In addition, research studies have shown that peer influence is one of the strongest methods of nurturing effective practice among teachers (e.g., Papay, Taylor, Tyler, & Laski, 2016). The image of a lone do-gooder is romantic, but it is just not feasible in the long run as a way to help all kids learn. Putting so much of a burden on one person will eventually lead to overload and burnout. Teaching entails building on the work and efforts of others, and such an endeavor requires many hands.

Consistency involves following through, making sure that there is a sense of fairness and justice in one's teaching. As we have discussed at length, students come to us with knowledge and expertise that often are overlooked. Those areas must be included in how we plan and execute our lessons if we want students to engage in learning in any meaningful way. And that must be carried out on a regular basis. Teaching is not effective when it is done piecemeal, and consistency helps students realize there is a structure and purpose in their education.

## CLOSING THOUGHTS

We have discussed, suggested, and modeled much over the course of this book, and in parting we provide a few important considerations we think are essential to keep in mind when teaching purposefully.

### For Teachers
- Don't stop learning. Stay informed about educational practice and research. Read. Seek out and participate in meaningful professional development.
- Find colleagues to trust and collaborate with. No one can be truly successful on his own.
- Take care of yourself, and don't be afraid to ask for help when needed. These both may be more easily said than done.

### For Departments/Teams
- Working together is in your best interests. Multiple heads are better than one for planning, carrying out consistently substantive instruction, and maintaining a sense of continuity across subjects and/or grade levels.
- Share resources and strategies with your colleagues. Chances are you will either rise or fall together.
- Provide mentors to help novice teachers along. Even someone who might seem prepared enough can benefit from another's experience. And vice versa.

### For Administrators
- Remember to also think like a teacher: Don't stop learning. Stay informed about educational practice and research. There are many programs and products out there, and you need to be a careful, critical consumer.

- Schedule time for teachers to meet, plan, and collaborate, and then respect that time. Certainly there is much that must be accomplished in a school day, but such teamwork can be highly productive in responding to students' needs and proactive in heading off later troubles.
- When evaluating teachers, keep in mind that responsive teaching will not always look the same. Students and teachers vary across grade levels, personality, and circumstance. What is fruitful or effective for one class or student may not be for another.

In a world where the only constants are diversity and change, our best recourse is to be informed, to prepare for multiple scenarios, to collaborate, and to rely on the support and efforts of others. Taking all of these considerations together, teachers can use responsive techniques to educate their students and also meet any reasonable set of academic standards at any level, any time—whether they are the Common Core State Standards, other current standards systems, or academic standards that will almost certainly be created in the future. By teaching on purpose, dear reader, you and your students will learn to not just meet those standards, but to consistently exceed them.

# References

Adler, M. (1998). *The Paideia proposal: An educational manifesto.* New York, NY: Touchstone.

Allington, R. (2007). Intervention all day long: New hope for struggling readers. *Voices from the Middle, 14*(4), 7–14.

Alvermann, D. E. (2001). Reading adolescents' reading identities: Looking back to see ahead. *Journal of Adolescent & Adult Literacy, 44*(8), 676–690.

Alvermann, D. (2005). Exemplary literacy instruction in grades 7–12: What counts and who's counting? In J. Flood & P. L. Anders (Eds.), *Literacy development of students in urban schools: Research and policy* (pp. 187–201). Newark, DE: International Reading Association.

Alvermann, D., Young, J., Weaver, D., Hinchman, K., Moore, D., Phelps, S., . . . Zalewski, P. (1996). Middle and high school students' perceptions of how they experience text-based discussions: A multicase study. *Reading Research Quarterly, 31*(3), 244–267.

Aukerman, M. S. (2007). When reading it wrong is getting it right: Shared evaluation pedagogy among struggling fifth grade readers. *Research in the Teaching of English, 42,* 56–103.

Bardach, E. (2005). *A practical guide to policy analysis: The eightfold path to more effective problem solving* (2nd ed.). Washington, DC: CQ Press.

Berliner, D. C., Glass, G. V, & Associates. (2014) *50 myths and lies that threaten America's public schools: The real crisis in education.* New York, NY: Teachers College Press.

Birch, D. (1993). *The king's chessboard.* New York, NY: Puffin Books.

Blythe, T., & Associates. (1998). *The teaching for understanding guide.* San Francisco, CA: Jossey-Bass.

Botzakis, S, & Burns. L. D. (2013, November). *(Re)inventing ELA classrooms Using standards, research, technology and media.* Paper presented at the meeting of the National Council of Teachers of English. Boston, MA.

Bruce, B. (2002). Diversity and critical social engagement: How changing technologies enable new modes of literacy in changing circumstances. In D. Alvermann (Ed.), *Adolescents and literacies in a digital world* (pp. 1–18). New York, NY: Peter Lang.

Burns, L. D. (2014). *Moving targets: A critical discourse analysis of standards and teacher preparation in English language arts.* Saarbrücken, Germany: Scholar's Press.

Burns, L. D., & Botzakis, S. (2012). Using *The Joy Luck Club* to teach core standards and 21st century literacies. *English Journal, 101*(5), 23–29.

Burns, L. D., & Miller, sj. (in press). Social justice policymaking in teacher education from conception to application: Realizing Standard VI. *Teachers College Record.*

Carter, C. (2009). Priest, prostitute, plumber? The construction of teachers as saints. *English Education, 42*(1), 61–90.

Center for Media Literacy. (2003). CML MediaLit kit: A framework for learning and teaching in a media age. Retrieved from www.medialit.org

Chandler-Olcott, K., & Mahar, D. (2003a). Adolescents' *anime*-inspired "fanfictions": An exploration of mulitliteracies. *Journal of Adolescent & Adult Literacy, 46*(7), 556–566.

Chandler-Olcott, K., & Mahar, D. (2003b). "Tech-savviness" meets multiliteracies: Exploring adolescent girls' technology-mediated literacy practices. *Reading Research Quarterly, 38*(3), 356–385.

Danielson, C. (1996). *Enhancing professional practice: A framework for teaching.* Alexandria, VA: Association for Supervision and Curriculum Development.

DBQ Project. (2015). The DBQ project. Retrieved from www.dbqproject.com/index.php

Dewey, J. (1938). *Experience and education.* New York, NY: Free Press.

Dewey, J. (1944). *Democracy and education.* New York, NY: Macmillan.

Doray, B. (1990). *From Taylorism to Fordism: A rational madness.* London, United Kingdom: Free Assn Books.

Edison, T. (2016). Purpose quotes. Retrieved from www.brainyquote.com/quotes/keywords/purpose.html

Fecho, B., & Amatucci, K. B. (2008). Spinning out of control: Dialogical transactions in an English classroom. *English Teaching: Practice and Critique, 7*(1), 5–21.

Fecho, B., & Botzakis, S. (2007). Feasts of becoming: Imagining a literacy classroom based on dialogic beliefs. *Journal of Adolescent & Adult Literacy, 50*(7), 548–558.

Feig, P., & Apatow, J. (2004). *Freaks and geeks: The complete scripts* (Vol. 1). New York, NY: New Market Press.

Franceschini, S., Gori, S., Ruffino, M., Viola, S., Molteni, M., & Facoetti, A. (2013). Action video games make dyslexic children read better. *Current Biology, 23*(6), 462–466.

Frank, A. (1993). *The diary of a young girl.* New York, NY: Bantam Books.

Friese, E., Alvermann, D., Parkes, A., & Rezak, A. (2008). Selecting texts for English language arts classrooms: When assessment is not enough. *English Teaching: Practice and Critique, 7*(3), 74–99.

Fusaro, M. (2008, May 29). What is teaching for understanding? Retrieved from https://www.gse.harvard.edu/news/uk/08/05/what-teaching-understanding

Gaver, W. W. (1991). Technology affordances. In S. P. Robertson, G. M. Olson, & J. S. Olson, (Eds.), *Proceedings of the ACM CHI 91 Human Factors in Computing Systems Conference April 28–June 5, 1991* (pp. 79–84). New York, NY: Association for Computing Machinery.

Gay, G. (2010). *Culturally responsive teaching: Research, theory, and practice.* New York, NY: Teachers College Press.

Gee, J. P. (2003). *What video games have to teach us about learning and literacy.* New York, NY: Palgrave Macmillan.

Ginott, H. (1993). *Teacher and child: A book for parents and teachers.* New York, NY: Scribner.

Gladwell, M. (2008). *Outliers: The story of success.* New York, NY: Little Brown.

Goldberg, K. (2007). *Using technology for problem solving in middle and high school mathematics.* Upper Saddle River, NJ: Pearson Education.

Golden, B., Grooms, J., Sampson, V., & Oliveri, R. (2012). Generating arguments about climate change. *Science Scope, 35*(7), 26–34.

Golden, J. (2001). *Reading in the dark: Using film as a tool in the English classroom.* Urbana, IL: National Council of Teachers of English.

Golding, W. (2012). *The lord of the flies.* New York, NY: Faber & Faber.

Graves, M. (2004). Theories and constructs that have made a significant difference in adolescent literacy—but have the potential to produce still more positive benefits. In T. Jetton & J. Dole (Eds.), *Adolescent literacy research and practice* (pp. 433–452). New York, NY: Guilford Press.

Green, P. (2014). The hard part. Retrieved from www.huffingtonpost.com/peter-greene/the-hardest-partteaching_b_5554448.html?utm_hp_ref=tw

Greenleaf, C., & Schoenbach, R. (2001). Apprenticing adolescent readers to academic literacy. *Harvard Education Review, 71*(1). Retrieved from readingapprenticeship.org/wp-content/uploads/2014/01/Apprenticing-Adolescent-Readers-Ac-Lit.pdf

Grisham, D., & Wolsey, T. (2006). Recentering the middle school classroom as a vibrant learning community: Students, literacy, and technology intersect. *Journal of Adolescent & Adult Literacy, 49*(8), 648–660.

Grolnick, W. S., & Ryan, R. M. (1987). Autonomy in children's learning: An experimental and individual difference investigation. *Journal of Personality and Social Psychology, 52,* 890–898.

Guthrie, J. (2002). Preparing students for high-stakes test taking in reading. In A. Farstrup & S. J. Samuels (Eds.), *What research has to say about reading instruction* (pp. 370–391). Newark, DE: International Reading Association.

Guthrie, J., & Alao, S. (1997). Designing contexts to increase motivation for reading. *Educational Psychologist, 32,* 95–107.

Guthrie, J. T., Alao, S., & Rinehart, J. (1997). Engagement for young adolescents. *Journal of Adolescent & Adult Literacy, 40*(6), 438–446.

Guthrie, J., Coddington, C., & Wigfield, A. (2009). Profiles of reading motivation among African American and Caucasian students. *Journal of Literacy Research, 41*(3), 317–353.

Guthrie, J., & Davis, M. (2003). Motivating struggling readers in middle school through an engagement model of classroom practice. *Reading and Writing Quarterly, 19*(1), 59–85.

Guthrie, J., Perencevich, K., Wigfield, A., Taboada, A., Humenick, N., & Barbosa, P. (2006). Influences of stimulating tasks on reading motivation and comprehension. *The Journal of Educational Research, 99*(4), 232–245.

Guthrie, J., & Wigfield, A. (2000). Engagement and motivation in reading. In M. L. Kamil, P. B. Mosenthal, P. D. Pearson, & R. Barr (Eds.), *Handbook of reading research* (Vol. 3, pp. 403–422). Mahwah, NJ: Erlbaum.

Gutierrez, K. D. (2008). Developing a sociocritical literacy in the Third Space. *Reading Research Quarterly, 43*(2), 148–164.

Hall, L. A., Burns, L. D., & Edwards, E. C. (2010). *Empowering struggling readers: Practices for the middle grades*. New York, NY: Guilford Press.

Hall, L.A., Burns, L. D., & Greene, H. T. (2013). Creating inclusive spaces for struggling readers. In E. Ortlieb & E. Cheek (Eds.), *School-based interventions for struggling readers, K–8: Literacy research, practice and evaluation* (Vol. 3, pp. 219–240). New York, NY: Emerald Group Publishing.

Harvey, S. (2002). Nonfiction inquiry: Using real reading and writing to explore the world. *Language Arts, 80*, 12–22.

The Hemingway Challenge. (2005, July/August). *Utne, 92*.

Hinds, G. (2010). *The odyssey: A graphic novel*. Somerville, MA: Candlewick Press.

Hobbs, R. (2007). *Reading the media: Media literacy in high school English*. New York, NY: Teachers College Press.

Hochschild, A. (1998). *King Leopold's ghost: A story of greed, terror, and heroism in colonial Africa*. Boston, MA: Houghton Mifflin.

Howe, N., & Strauss, W. (2009). *Millennials rising: The next great generation*. New York, NY: Vintage Books.

Howley, K. (2007). Reading reality television: Cultivating critical media literacy. In M. T. Christel & S. Sullivan (Eds.), *Lesson plans for creating media-rich classrooms* (pp. 148–155). Urbana, IL: National Council of Teachers of English.

Hruby, G., Burns, L., Botzakis, S., Groenke, S., Laughter, J., & Hall, L. (in press). Agency in education: An abbreviated centennial history of motivation and engagement theory in literacy research. *Review of Research in Education*.

Hunter, M. C. (1982). *Mastery teaching*. El Segundo, CA: Tip Publications.

Ivey, G., & Broaddus, K. (2001). "Just plain reading": A survey of what makes students want to read in middle school classrooms. *Reading Research Quarterly, 36*, 350–377.

Jackson, P. (1990). *Life in classrooms*. New York, NY: Teachers College Press.

Jacobs, D. (2007). More than words: Comics as a means of teaching multiple literacies. *English Journal, 96*(3), 19–25.

Johnson, H., & Freedman, L. (2005). *Developing critical awareness at the middle level: Using texts as tools for critique and pleasure*. Newark, DE: International Reading Association.

Johnston, P., & Costello, P. (2005). Principles for literacy assessment. *Reading Research Quarterly, 4*(2), 256–267.

Kim, H., & Kamil, M. (2004). Adolescents, computer technology, and literacy. In T. Jetton & J. Dole (Eds.), *Adolescent literacy research and practice* (pp. 351–368). New York, NY: Guilford Press.

Kipling, R. (1899). The White man's burden. Retrieved from public.wsu.edu/~brians/world_civ/worldcivreader/world_civ_reader_2/kipling.html

Kist, W. (2005). *New literacies in action: Teaching and learning in multiple media*. New York, NY: Teachers College Press.

Klem, A., & Connell, P. (2004, March). *Relationships matter: Linking teacher support to student engagement and achievement*. Paper presented at the 10th biennial meeting of the Society for Research on Adolescence, Baltimore, MD.

Kottke, S. (2008, December). *RSVPs to reading: Gendered responses to the permeable curriculum*. Paper presented at the National Reading Conference, Orlando, FL.

Lanham, R. A. (2001). What's next for text? *Education, Communication & Information, 1*(1), 15–36.

Lenters, K. (2006). Resistance, struggle, and the adolescent reader. *Journal of Adolescent & Adult Literacy, 50*(2), 136–146.

Littler, C. R. (1978). Understanding Taylorism. *The British Journal of Sociology, 29*(2), 185–202.

Lloyd, G., Beckmann, S., Zbiek, R. M., & Cooney, T. (2010). *Developing essential understanding of functions for teaching mathematics in grades 9–12.* Reston, VA: National Council of Teachers of Mathematics.

Lortie, D. (1975). *Schoolteacher: A sociological study.* Chicago, IL: University of Chicago Press.

Madden, M., Lenhart, A., Duggan, M., Cortesi, S., & Gasser, U. (2013). *Teens and technology 2013.* Pew Internet & American Life Project and Harvard's Berkman Society for Internet & Society Retrieved from www.pewinternet.org/2013/03/13/teens-and-technology-2013/

Manguel, A. (1997). *The history of reading.* New York: Penguin.

Marsh, J. (2006). Popular culture in the literacy curriculum: A Bourdieuan analysis. *Reading Research Quarterly, 41*(2), 160–174.

Marzano, R., Pickering, D., & Pollock, J. (2001). *Classroom instruction that works: Research-based strategies for increasing student achievement.* Upper Saddle River, NJ: Prentice Hall.

McCloud, S. (1993). *Understanding comics: The invisible art.* Northampton, MA: Tundra.

McGinnis, T. (2007). Khmer rap boys, X-Men, Asia's fruits, and Dragonball Z: Creating multilingual and multimodal classroom contexts. *Journal of Adolescent & Adult Literacy, 50*(7), 570–579.

McTighe, J., & Wiggins, G. (2013). *Essential questions: Opening doors to student understanding.* Alexandria, VA: Association for Supervision and Curriculum Development.

Meier, D., & Wood, G. (2004). *Many children left behind: How the No Child Left Behind Act is damaging our children and our schools.* Boston, MA: Beacon Press.

Moje, E. (2008). Foregrounding the disciplines in secondary literacy teaching and learning: A call for change. *Journal of Adolescent & Adult Literacy, 52*(2), 96–107.

Moje, E., Ciechanowski, K. M., Kramer, L., Ellis, L., Carrillo, R., & Collazo, T. (2004). Working toward Third Space in content area literacy: An examination of everyday funds of knowledge and discourse. *Reading Research Quarterly, 39*(1), 38–70.

Moll, L., Amanti, C., Neff, D., & Gonzalez, N. (1992). Funds of knowledge for teaching: A qualitative approach to connect homes and classrooms. *Theory into Practice, 31*(2), 132–141.

Moll, L., & Gonzalez, N. (2001). Lessons from research with language-minority children. In E. Cushman, E. Kintgen, B. Kroll, & M. Rose (Eds.), *Literacy: A critical sourcebook* (pp. 156–172). New York, NY: Bedford/St. Martins.

Monnin, K. (2009). Finding literacy in Neverland. *Voices from the Middle, 16*(3), 54–56.

Morel, E. D. (1903). The Black man's burden. Retrieved from www.csun.edu/~jaa7021/hist434/Morel.pdf

Nash, R. (2012). *Teacher expectations and student learning.* New York, NY: Routledge.

National Council for the Social Studies. (2013). *College, career, and civic life: C3 framework for social studies standards.* Silver Spring, MA: Author.

National Council of Teachers of English. (1996). *Guidelines for the preparation of teachers of English language arts, grades 7–12.* Urbana IL: Author.

National Council of Teachers of English. (2014). Why class size matters today. Retrieved from www.ncte.org/positions/statements/why-class-size-matters

National Council of Teachers of Mathematics. (2009). Focus on high school mathematics: Reason and Sense Making. Reston, VA: National Council of Teachers of Mathematics.

National Governors Association Center for Best Practices, Council of Chief State School Officers. (2010). English language arts standards>>introduction>>key design considerations. Retrieved from www.corestandards.org/ELA-Literacy/introduction/key-design-consideration/

Nelson, H. (2013). *Testing more, teaching less: What America's obsession with student testing costs in money and lost instructional time.* Washington, DC: American Federation of Teachers.

New London Group. (1996). A pedagogy of multiliteracies: Designing social futures. *Harvard Educational Review, 66*(1), 60–92.

O'Brien, D. (2001, June). "At-risk" adolescents: Redefining competence through the multiliteracies of intermediality, visual arts, and representation. *Reading Online, 4*(11).

Oldfather, P., & Dahl, K. (1994). Toward a social constructivist reconceptualization of intrinsic motivation for literacy learning. *Journal of Reading Behavior, 26*(2), 139–158.

Orwell, G. (1981). *A collection of essays.* San Diego, CA: Harcourt Brace Jovanovich.

Otis, N., Grouzet, F., & Pelletier, L. (2005). Latent motivational change in an academic setting: A 3-year longitudinal study. *Journal of Educational Psychology, 97*(2), 170–183.

Papay, J. P., Taylor, E. S., Tyler, J. H., & Laski, M. (2016, February). *Learning job skills from colleagues at work: Evidence from a field experiment using teacher performance data* (Working Paper). Retrieved from www.newyorkfed.org/medialibrary/media/research/education_seminar_series/pttl-learning-from-colleagues.pdf

Perkins, D. (1995). *Smart schools: From training memories to educating minds.* New York, NY: Simon & Schuster.

Poe, E. A. (1983). *The pit and the pendulum.* New York, NY: Bantam Classics.

Quinn, D. (n.d.). If a doctor . . . Retrieved from blog.gaiam.com/quotes/authors/donald-quinn/60742

RAND Corporation. (2014). Teaching matters: Understanding teachers' impact on student achievement. Retrieved from www.rand.org/education/projects/measuring-teacher-effectiveness/teachers-matter.html

Reed, J., Shallert, D., Beth, A., & Woodruff, A. (2004). Motivated reader, engaged writer: The role of motivation in the literate acts of adolescents. In T. Jetton & J. Dole (Eds.), *Adolescent literacy research and practice* (pp. 251–282). New York, NY: Guilford Press.

Reeve, J., & Jang, H. (2006). What teachers say and do to support students' autonomy during a learning activity. *Journal of Educational Psychology, 98*(1), 209–218.

Risko, V., & Walker-Dalhouse, D. (2007). Tapping students' cultural funds of knowledge to address the achievement gap. *The Reading Teacher, 61*(1), 98–100.

Rosenthal, R. (2002). The Pygmalion effect and its mediating mechanisms. In J. Aronson (Ed.), *Improving academic achievement: Impact of psychological factors on education* (pp. 25–36). San Diego, CA: Academic Press.

Roth, V. (2011). *Divergent*. New York, NY: HarperCollins.

Rothstein, D., & Santana, L. (2011). *Make just one change: Teach students to ask their own questions*. Cambridge, MA: Harvard Education Press.

Sagan, C. (2011). *Demon-haunted world: Science as a candle in the dark*. New York, NY: Random House.

Salinger, J. D. (2008). *The catcher in the rye*. New York, NY: Paw Prints.

Sampson, V., Grooms, J., & Walker, J. P. (2011). Argument driven inquiry as a way to help students learn how to participate in scientific argumentation and craft written arguments: An exploratory study. *Science Education, 95*(2), 217–257.

Scherff, L., & Piazza, L. (2008). Why now, more than ever, we need to talk about opportunity to learn. *Journal of Adolescent & Adult Literacy, 52*(4), 343–352.

Schiefele, U. (1996). Topic interest, text representation, and quality of experience. *Contemporary Educational Psychology, 21*, 3–18.

Schraw, G. (1997). Situational interest in literary text. *Contemporary Educational Psychology, 22*(4), 436–456.

Schraw, G., Flowerday, T., & Reisetter, M. F. (1998). The role of choice in reader engagement. *Journal of Educational Psychology, 90*(4), 705–714.

Shakespeare, W. (2009). *Julius Caesar: The Cambridge Dover Wilson Shakespeare*. Cambridge, United Kingdom: Cambridge University Press.

Shick, N., & Hierl, W. (2007). *AP United States history teacher's guide*. Atlanta, GA: College Board.

Skinner, E. A., & Belmont, M. J. (1993). Motivation in the classroom: Reciprocal effects of teacher behavior and student engagement across the school year. *Journal of Educational Psychology, 85*(4), 571–581.

Smith, M. J., & Burston, W. H. (Eds.). (1983). *Chrestomathia: Collected works of Jeremy Bentham*. London, United Kingdom: Oxford University Press.

Spielvogel, J. J. (2009). *Western civilization*. Southbank, Victoria, Australia: Thomson Learning Australia.

Spires, H. A., & Donley, J. (1998). Prior knowledge activation: Inducing engagement with informational texts. *Journal of Educational Psychology, 90*(2), 249–260.

Steele, C. (2011). *Whistling Vivaldi: How stereotypes affect us and what we can do*. New York, NY: Norton.

Steinkuehler, C. (2010). Video games and digital literacies. *Journal of Adolescent & Adult Literacy, 54*(1), 61–63.

Stone, D. (2002). *Policy paradox: The art of political decision making* (Rev. ed.). New York, NY: Norton.

Street, B. (2003). What's "new" in New Literacy Studies? Critical approaches to literacy in theory and practice. *Current Issues in Comparative Education, 5*(2), 77–91.

Thoman, E., & Jolls, T. (2004). Media literacy—A national priority for a changing world. *American Behavioral Scientist, 48*(1), 18–29.

Thomas, S., & Oldfather, P. (1997). Intrinsic motivations, literacy, and assessment practices: "That's my grade. That's me." *Educational Psychologist, 32*(2), 107–123.

Twain, M. (1992). *Collected tales, sketches, speeches, & essays, 1852–1890* (L. J. Budd, Ed.). New York, NY: Library of America.

Tyack, D., & Cuban, L. (1995). *Tinkering toward utopia: A century of public school reform.* Cambridge, MA: Harvard University Press.

Walker, A. (1973). Everyday use. In *In love and trouble* (pp. 47–59). New York, NY: Harcourt Brace.

Weinstein, S. (2007). A love for the thing: The pleasures of rap as a literate practice. *Journal of Adolescent & Adult Literacy, 50*(4), 270–281.

Wentzel, K. (1997). Student motivation in middle school: The role of perceived pedagogical caring. *Journal of Educational Psychology, 89*(3), 411–419.

Wigfield, A. (1997). Reading motivation: A domain-specific approach to motivation. *Educational Psychologist, 32*(2), 59–68.

Wiggins, G. P., & McTighe, J. (2005). *Understanding by design.* Alexandria, VA: Association for Supervision and Curriculum Development.

Wiggins, G. P., & Wilbur, D. (2015). How to make your questions essential. *Educational Leadership, 73*(1), 10–15.

Yang, G. (2008). Graphic novels in the classroom. *Language Arts, 85*(3), 185–192.

Young, J. (2000). Boy talk: Critical literacy and masculinities. *Reading Research Quarterly, 35*(3), 312–337.

# Index

# About the Authors

**Leslie David Burns** is associate professor of literacy and program chair of English education for the Department of Curriculum and Instruction at the University of Kentucky, and winner of the Edward Fry Book Award from the Literacy Research Association.

**Stergios Botzakis** is associate professor of literacy education at the University of Tennessee, Knoxville, and is known for his work in multimodal literacies.

**Maureen Cavalcanti** is a former secondary grades mathematics teacher and current doctoral student in education sciences with the department of STEM education at the University of Kentucky.

**Barry W. Golden** is an assistant professor of science education at the University of Tennessee, Knoxville, and is known for his work on climate literacy and the nature of science.

**Ryan New** was the 2014 Kentucky Council for Social Studies High School Teacher of the Year. He teaches AP world history, AP government and politics, and U.S. history at Boyle County High School in Danville, Kentucky, and is a doctoral student in curriculum and instruction at the University of Kentucky.

**Katie Raby** is currently a 9th-grade English language arts teacher at Grace Christian Academy, and she formerly taught high school English at Hardin Valley Academy in Knoxville, TN.